The Wisdom of the East

EDITED BY J. L. CRANMER-BYNG M.C.

A FURTHER SELECTION FROM THE THREE HUNDRED POEMS OF THE T'ANG DYNASTY

A Further Selection from the

THREE HUNDRED POEMS
OF THE T'ANG DYNASTY

translated by

SOAME JENYNS

Deputy Keeper, Dept. of Oriental Antiquities
at the British Museum

Chu Sun, comp.

John Murray
50 Albemarle Street
London.

For Anne

WHO HELPED TO CHOOSE THEM

First Edition June 1944
Reprinted July 1944
Reprinted June 1945
Reprinted March 1948
Reprinted July 1959

Made and Printed in Great Britain
by Butler & Tanner Ltd.
Frome and London

CONTENTS

5

Poems by

Editorial Note

The object of the Editor of this series is a very definite one. He desires above all things that these books shall be the ambassadors of good-will between East and West. He hopes that they will contribute to a fuller knowledge of the great cultural heritage of the East, for only through real understanding will the West be able to appreciate the underlying problems and aspirations of Asia to-day. He is confident that a deeper knowledge of the great ideals and lofty philosophy of Eastern thought will help to a revival of that true spirit of charity which neither despises nor fears the nations of another creed and colour.

J. L. CRANMER-BYNG

50 *Albemarle Street*
  *London, W.*1

AUTHOR'S NOTE

I AM delighted that the public interest in the first volume of selections from the Three Hundred Poems of the T'ang Dynasty has been sufficient to raise a demand for a second selection.

This second selection includes practically all the poems in that anthology which remain worth printing.

In this volume there has been no attempt to muster the poems by theme, but an index places them under their authors.

I should have liked to have included a few biographical notes on the T'ang poets themselves, but the war has not permitted the time to collect these.

As I have dealt at length with the background to the poetry of the T'ang dynasty in the introduction to my previous volume, I feel that I have exhausted this subject and would refer those who are interested to the preface in question.

The Song of never-ending Grief [1]

by PO CHÜ-I

THE Chinese Emperor, obsessed by beauty longed for one who
    might subvert the kingdom [2]

In the Imperial palace he sought for many years but could not
    find her.

The Yang family had a daughter scarcely grown up

Brought up in the depths of the women's apartments,

Unknown to anyone outside [3]

Heaven had endowed her with graces that she herself could not
    disdain.

One day she is chosen to stand by the Emperor's side,

At the turn of her eyes, at the flash of her smile a hundred
    compliments are born ;

Who of the powdered and pencilled favourites of the six palaces
    can compete with such beauty ?

At the Imperial behest in the cool springtime she washes in the
    Hua-ch'ing [4] pool ;

Smooth and warm the fountain water washes her alabaster [5]
    skin

The attendant maid supports languid loveliness

---

[1] This poem refers to the love of the Emperor Hsüan Tsung, known as
Ming Huang (the Magnificent), for his concubine Yang Kuei-fei, for
whom he neglected his kingdom. The revolt of An Lu-shan forced
him to flee with her to Szechwan, where his own troops threatened to
mutiny unless Yang Kuei-fei was removed. She was allowed to strangle
herself.

    Translated Giles, *Chinese Literature* p. 169 *et seq.*, *The Everlasting Wrong*.

[2] The literal translation is a " Kingdom breaker." This is a stock epithet
of extreme beauty. Hsüan Tsung did not wish to have his Kingdom
subverted !

[3] She had already been the concubine of the Emperor's son Prince Shao
before she received imperial favours.

[4] Pool of Flowering Purity.

[5] Literally " like congealed ointment," *Odes* I, 5, 3, S. 2.

From this time the new arrival enjoys Imperial favour
Her cloud front coiffure, her painted face
Her hair ornaments,[1] which swing as she walks
She spends the warm spring night within the hibiscus bed curtains ;
Ah ! How far too fleeting was that spring night and how early the rising of the sun,
From this time onwards the Emperor gives no early audience.
She receives his favours and she waits on him at his feasts without break
She is always chosen for the spring excursion ; chosen for the nightly carouse.
In the palace there are three thousand beauties,
But the favour that should have been extended to three thousand
Is concentrated on the person of one.
In her " Golden Home " she beauties herself to attend him in the evening
The feasts of the jade tower ended
She turns to him delirious with love.
Brothers and sisters, all are raised to noble rank ;
Alas ! for the ill-omened [2] glories of the house in which she was born ;
From this time onwards a parent's wish was not for the birth of sons, but of daughters.
The palace of Li towers into the azure sky
Fairy music is wafted on the breeze and is heard all round
Languid chanting and slow dancing linger to the sound of guitar and flute,
All day long the Emperor gazes upon her with never satiated eyes.

[1] Literally " gold step sway." A kind of shimmering head-dress ; in her case made of gold.

[2] Her brother, who became Prime Minister, and her two sisters, who became ladies of the court, were destroyed with her.

From Yü-yang [1] comes the roll of drums that makes the earth
    tremble.
Fear scatters the song of the " Rainbow Skirt and the Feathered
    Jacket." [2]
From the nine-towered gate towers smoke and dust rise
A thousand chariots, ten thousand horsemen go to the south-
    west,
Swaggering plumes go onwards, then halt.
From the gates of the capital they have gone a day's journey to
    the west
The six armies will go no further, there is no help for it
To appease them the moth-like eyebrows [3] must die before their
    horses,
Flower-like jewellery is thrown to the ground and no one picks
    it up
Kingfisher feather work, golden birds and hairpins of jade lie
    there unclaimed,
The Emperor buries his face and cannot save her,
He looks back on the place where her blood and his tears flowed
    together.
The yellow dust is blown far and wide and the wind blows
    bleak and cold
From " Cloudy Pass " the road turns and winds up to the
    Sword Shelf.
Few walk beneath the shadow of Omei Shan,
The gleam of their banners is darkened ; the sun is dimmed.
Oh ! Jade-like are the streams of Szechwan, green are its
    hills !
The monarch morning and evening is overcome by his feelings
Gazing on the moon from his temporary palace its beauty hurts
    him

[1] In Chihli.
[2] A dance that the Emperor Hsüan Tsung is supposed to have been
taught in a dream by Ch'ang-o, the Goddess of the Moon, and which he
had put to music for Yang Kuei-fei.
[3] i.e. Yang Kuei-fei.

In the evening rain he hears the tinkling of bells and his heart melts.

There is a change of fortune, the days go by the Emperor returns;

When he arrives at the place (where she died) nerveless and irresolute, he cannot go on;

On the slopes of Ma-wei there are but stretches of mud,

He cannot see the jade face in the empty place of death.

The Emperor and his ministers regard each other and their clothes are wet (with tears).

Eastwards towards the gates of the capital their horses bear them as they will,

Once home they find the ponds and gardens all as before;

By the T'ai-i Lake the hibiscus are open and by the Wei-yang Palace the willows are in bud,

The hibiscus flowers are like her face, the willow buds like her eyebrows.

When he is faced by such beauty he cannot refrain from tears.

The spring wind sways the blossom of peach and plum

The autumn rain brings down the leaves from the Wu-t'ung tree,

In the southern enclosure of the western palace the autumn colours the grass,[1]

The fallen leaves cover the terraces with red but no one sweeps them away.

The actors of the "pear garden"[2] have aged

The eunuchs of the "pepper room"[3] have lost their charm,

At night in the hall the flitting fireflies remind him of his sorrow

The wick of his single lamp is burnt to the rind,

Still sleep does not come;

Throughout the long night he hears drums and bells mark the slowly passing hours

Gradually the Milky Way yields to the dawn,

[1] Lit. "The autumn touched foliage is abundant."
[2] The famous theatrical school founded by Ming Huang.
[3] Part of the palace devoted to the eunuchs.

The mandarin duck and drake tiles [1] glitter coldly in the hoar
    frost,
The Emperor is cold beneath the kingfisher quilt
For who is there to share it with him?
Slowly, sadly, a year rolls by since dead and living were parted
Her ghost does not come back to haunt his dreams.
In Ling ch'iung [1] there is a famous Taoist priest, in the Record
    Office,
Who is able by earnest concentration to summon the in-
    habitants of the ghostly world.
As the Emperor rolls from side to side distracted by his thoughts
They cause the priest to concentrate his powers in search;
He mounts up into space and rides the ether, rushing with speed
    of lightning
Up to heaven and down to earth searching on every hand,
Above he exhausts the blue heavens, below he exhausts the
    yellow springs
But in neither of these vast areas can he find her.
Suddenly he hears that on the sea there is a fairy island mountain.
This mountain floats in space amidst the void
Towards dwellings hung with tinkling bells;
Five-coloured clouds envelop it
Amidst it all the children of the immortal world move gracefully
    to and fro;
Among the others there dwells T'ai-chên [3]
By her snowy skin and her flower-like face he has a feeling that
    it must be she.
To the west of the gold palace is a courtyard
He knocks at the jade gate and asks Hsiao-yü [4] to let Shuang-
    ch'êng know.

   [1] The mandarin duck and drake were symbolical of conjugal faithful-
ness. They were supposed to mate for life and that one could never
survive the other.
   [2] Szechwan.
   [3] T'ai-chên and Shuang Ch'êng names of endearment for Yang Kuei-
fei.
   [4] Hsiao-yü was Yang Kuei-fei's maid.

Hearing of a messenger that has arrived from the Emperor
The nine embroidered bed-curtains are pulled aside and the
   sleeping ghost starts up.
Grasping her clothes she pushes aside the pillow and rises in a
   flutter
Pearl-studded blinds and silver screens are drawn to one side
Her cloud-like hair is disarranged as she comes straight from
   her slumbers,
Her flowing head-dress is not straight as she comes down the hall
The wind blows the fairy sleeves hither and thither as she
   comes
As if once more she danced to the tunes of the Rainbow Skirt
   and the Feathered Jacket.
Her jadelike face is drawn and sad
Her tears drop on the balcony,
A spray of pear blossom is drenched as with spring rain
Yet her passions are controlled though the tears stand in her
   eyes as she thanks the Emperor's messenger
Since their separation from each other both appearance and
   voice have grown indistinct.
In the Chao-yang Hall his love and benevolence will never reach
   her again
In fairyland days and months are long.
Turning her head she can gaze down at the world of men
But she cannot see Chang-an because of the mists and dust ;
All she can do is to bring old toys, tokens of their great love,
The gold and enamel box and hairpin, these she sends to him
From the pin she reserves a piece, of the box she retains the lid.
She breaks the yellow gold of the pin, she divides the box
To signify her heart is as true as the gold and enamel pin [1]
Whether it is in this world or the next they meet again.
When the messenger is about to go
She emphasizes her messages
Among them recalling a pledge which they two alone know
How on the seventh day of the seventh month

[1] " To bid his heart be firm as the gold and enamel pin."

When at midnight they were alone in the Ch'ang-shêng Palace
   they whispered these words :
" We swear that in the sky we will be like one-winged birds
   (that must fly together)
And on earth like trees with interlocked branches."
Both heaven and earth must pass away in due course
But this wrong shall stretch out for ever without an end.

Sad Thoughts (an allegory) [1]

by CHANG CHIU-LING

Part I

THE lonely swan comes over the sea
But she does not dare to look back on the marshes,
With a side glance she sees two kingfisher birds
That nest in the three pearl trees ; [2]
High up among the woods on the precious peaks.
How is it that they do not fear the archer's metal ?

---

[1] This class of allegorical poems forms a regular category called Kan Yü.
We are told that those of Ch'ên Tzŭ-ang were profound while those of
Chang Chiu-ling were refined ; both followed the style of Yüan Chi
(see Giles, *Biographical Dict.*, No. 2544).

This poem is not really one poem in four parts but four poems that
reflect four different phases of the poet's mind. They were written after
the author had been forced out of office by Niu Hsien-k'o and Li Lin-fu
and their manner supports an allegorical interpretation. The writer
compares himself to a solitary wild swan and a remote orange tree and
his enemies to the brilliant kingfishers. The first part contains almost
a touch of triumph in renunciation, which gives way in the second to
the philosophic solace of self-fulfilment. The third part reveals a definite
sense of frustration, which in the last is succeeded by a feeling of bitterness
and resignation.

[2] North of Yin city by the red water is supposed to have grown a
mythical tree like a cedar with leaves of pearls ; here an indirect allusion
to the court.

The less fortunate point at their beautiful clothes,
For the powerful must be careful to avoid jealousy.
To-day I roam the solitary wastes,[1]
How should the hunters want to shoot at me?

Part II

In spring the delicate shoots of the orchid push forth again[2]
In autumn the cassia blossoms (open) in their dazzling purity,
Each rejoices in its own vital essence
And each has its own season.
Who knows (the thoughts of) the hermit who lives in the
    woods?
He hears the wind soughing in the trees and is happy,
Grass and tree do not seek to be transplanted
Do they beg fair maidens to pluck them?[3]

Part III

The recluse returns home and lies down in peace,
His banked-up cares are washed away,
He has broken with high-flying ambition
And passed on to the peace of remote obscurity.
Day and night I nurse my solitary thoughts.
Who can besmirch my loftiness of soul?
The fish who bore down to the depths and the birds that fly
    up to the heavens have nothing in common.
How can I fail to be comforted by my sincerity of mind?[4]

Part IV

South of the Yangtze there red oranges grow
Right through the winter they are still a green forest,

[1] i.e. Like the allegorical swan.
[2] More literally, are resplendent.
[3] A contrast to the Gray's *Elegy* idea of wasted sweetness.
[4] This line seems to show that after all he had not attained the detachment that he claimed.

This is not because they grow in a warm climate
But because they can endure the winter.
They might be set before the honoured guest.
Ah ! how come they to be hidden in deep valleys ?
Our destiny is determined by circumstance ;
What must be must be.
You talk only of planting the peach and the plum
Can this (orange) tree give no shade ? [1]

Gazing at a View of T'ai Shan [2]

by TU FU

T'AI Shan, what shall I say about you ?
To the front of you Ch'i,[3] behind you Lu [3]
Green as far as the eye can see ;
Heaven and earth unite in you their spiritual grace.
(Around your peaks) the Yin and Yang [4] divide dusk from dawn.
Your piled up clouds purge my feelings,
My straining eye can (scarcely) follow your birds into their nests.
If I climb the mountain to its summits
Hills stretch away beneath me on every side.

[1] To insist on planting only the peach or plum for shade is a foolish prejudice. The orange tree (the author) is perfectly capable of giving it, only its chance has not come.

[2] T'ai Shan, near T'ai-an in Shantung, is one of the five sacred hills of the Taoists. It represents the Eastern Quarter. In China the worship of mountains is immemorial.

[3] Two ancient dukedoms.

[4] The two primordial essences of Chinese philosophy into which all nature is divided. Yang the positive masculine principle corresponding to light, heat and the heavens, and Yin the negative feminine principle corresponding to darkness, cold and the earth.

A Presentation to Wei Pa, a retired Scholar

by TU FU

FRIENDSHIPS are made only to be broken.[1]
Orion far from Lucifer must shine.
Strange to-night of all nights
We should (sit) together by the light of the same candle.
Youth and strength, how long do they last?
My beard and hair are both already grizzled.
Visiting ancient friends I find half of them among the ghosts,
But now I meet you my heart is warmed.[2]
How was I to know that I should have to wait twenty years
Before I could revisit your home?
When we last parted you were not married;
Now all of a sudden I find you with a family of sons and
    daughters;
Politely and with looks of pleasure they wait on their father's
    old friend
Asking me from where I come.
We have not yet come to the end of our questions and answers,
(When) you bid the youngsters bring wine and set it before us.
Spring onions are cut in the evening rain
And are cooked fresh with yellow millet.
The host discourses of how difficult it is to bring about a meeting
And pledges me again and again;
Even after ten cups we are not drunk
Only we have become sentimental over our reminiscences.[3]
To-morrow the Western Hills will divide us,
And the affairs of the world
Will make us dim to each other.

[1] Perhaps too drastic; a better reading—" In life friends cannot often meet."

[2] Fletcher (*Gems of Chinese Verse*, p. 52) translates this " The sudden news catches the thrilling heart," apparently referring to the news of old friends.

[3] An alternative reading—" So grateful am I for your cherishing of old friendship."

The Blue Mountain Torrent

by WANG WEI

IT is said that those who make for the Yellow Flower River
Must pursue this blue mountain stream ;
And follow a myriad twists and turns among the hill ravines
Although as the crow flies the distance is less than a hundred
    miles.
The stream bickers among the pebbles and (under) the deep
    tranquil green of the pines,
Here broadening out to allow the water chestnut and water
    gentian to float on its surface,
And there glistening deep and bright among reeds and rushes.
I am by temperament indolent and slothful
And how much more by this restful clear stream ;
Leave me to ponder on the hermit's rock
For there dangling a fishing rod I am entirely content.

The Song of Hsi Shih [1]

by WANG WEI

THROUGHOUT the world beauty is a snare [2] to men
How could Hsi Shih long remain in obscurity ?
In the morning she was (washing clothes) by the river of Yüeh,[3]

[1] Hsi Shih, who is said to have lived in the fifth century B.C., was one
of the six famous Chinese beauties. She was of humble parentage and
gained her livelihood by washing clothes and selling firewood. She is
supposed to have suffered from heart trouble and when she was distressed
she knitted her eyebrows and this made her even more beautiful than
before. Reports of her loveliness reached a Prince of Yüeh who, on
the advice of his minister Fan Li, determined to use her to throw off the
tributary yoke of a Prince of Wu. To this end she was trained for three
years and then sent with a trousseau as a present to the Prince of Wu,
who was so infatuated by her beauty that he gave himself up to dissipation
in her company and was defeated by his neighbour.

[2] Literally, " valued by men."   [3] Chekiang.

In the evening she was a palace concubine of the King of
    Wu.[1]
When she was obscure how could she shine among the crowd?
When the hour of greatness came
Then at last her rare beauty was valued by men;
Attendants at her bidding wait on her with fragrant ointments
She no longer has to put on her own clothes,
Sunning herself in her sovereign's smile her airs and graces grow
    apace.
In the Prince's eyes she can do no wrong
Her erstwhile comrades of the wash-tub cannot ride home with
    her in the same chair.[2]
The daughters of neighbours must have it politely pointed out
    to them
That although they copy her frowns what hope have they?

Sent to Chang Wu on Climbing the Orchid Hill [3] in Autumn

by MÊNG HAO-JAN

HERE on the north peak among the white clouds
You enjoy the hermit's life,
And now in my yearning to reach you
I climb these high hills;
My heart follows the wild goose till
She disappears into space.
I am sad because the evening is coming on
I am happy because of the freshness of autumn;
From here I can see the farmers returning home
Walking along the sandy river bed till they rest at the head of
    the ford.
The trees on the horizon are like small herbs;
The island on the river looks like a moon.

[1] Kiangsu.   [2] Home, i.e. to the Prince of Wu's.
[3] Lan Shan in Kansu.

20

I wonder when we shall be able to bring wine to such a place as
    this?
Here having drunk together we could enjoy the autumn
    festival.[1]

*With my Brother in the Southern Studio enjoying the Moon and
thinking of Ts'ui, sub-prefect of Shan-yin* [2]

by WANG CH'ANG-LING

As I lie forgetful of worldly cares in the Southern Pavilion
I draw back the curtain to see the rising moon.
Tranquil waters and woodland lie bathed in the glorious
    moonlight
The shadows dance on the (paper) windows.
The moon waxes and wanes without end
As the present gives way to the past.
Meanwhile a virtuous friend sits by a clear river
This very evening humming some plaintive song of the South.
What matters it though hundreds of miles divide us?
The fragrance of orchids and azaleas [3] is carried all the way by
    the gentle breeze.

Floating on the Jo-yeh [4] *Stream in Spring*
by CH'I WU-CH'IEN

HERE is seclusion and stillness with nothing to break the spell;
We follow wherever the boat chooses to drift;
The evening wind wafts it on its way

[1] This festival is known as the "double nine" because it is observed
on the ninth day of the ninth month. The occasion is celebrated by a
trip to the hills, the gathering of hellebore and dogwood, which are
inimicable to evil spirits, and by the drinking of aster wine: kites are
flown and picnics are made.

[2] In Chekiang.

[3] An allegorical reference to the fame of his official friend.

[4] In Chekiang.

21

Entering the mouth of the gorge between flowery paths,
As dusk falls we wind among the western ravines.
Through a break in the hills one can see the Southern Dipper.
The air is heavy with floating mist
The moon among the trees sinks at my back.
The life of the world of men is a boundless waste ; [1]
My wish is to spend my days here as a fisherman in wild places.

On Stopping the Night with the Hermit Wang Ch'ang-ling

by CH'ANG CHIEN

CLEAN mountain streams are deep, and not to be measured
Where the hermit dwells alone with the passing clouds.
Through the firs peers the moon
Clear and bright especially on your account.
The thatched hut shelters the sleeping shadow of flowers,
The herb garden is deep with variegated mosses.
I also will say farewell to the world
And live on the Western Hill among the stork and phœnix.

I point out to the Officials even Thieves have Mercy

by YÜAN CHIEH

IN 763 bandits from the Western Plain entered Tao Chou.[2]
They burnt, slaughtered and ravaged till the district was almost
bare, and then left. The next year they attacked Yung [2] and
destroyed Shao,[2] but they did not attack this place, though they
came to its borders they went away ! How can it be said we
had the strength to oppose them. They pitied our plight, that
was why. You officers, why do you then oppress with heavy
taxes. It is for this reason I pen these verses to point out (your
errors).

[1] One commentary says, " is boundless like the expanse of water,"
but you can scarcely call a stream in a gorge boundless.
[2] Hunan.

In former years tranquility reigned.
For twenty years I lived among the wooded hills
A spring flowed before my house,
Peaceful ravines stretched away before my front door.
The land taxes were levied at fixed times.
In those days people could sleep freely.
Suddenly there came unrest
For several years I found myself in the imperial army
Now I come to be magistrate of this region.
The mountain barbarians ravage the land
But the bandits do not come to butcher our small city.
They pity our poverty,
And so they move on to attack neighbouring regions.
This district alone entirely is safe.
You officials who hold the royal warrant
Why are you not as good as they?
To-day the tax collectors crush the people
Roasting them over the fire (of their exactions).
Who will have the strength to come to their rescue
And become the hero of the age?
My wish is to hand over my tally
To take a pole and push off my boat
Moving my family to where they shall live on fish and grain,
And the home of my old age will be beside the lakes and rivers.

*Feasting a company of Scholars on a Rainy Day at Government
House*

by WEI YING-WU

THE well-disciplined guard put up their spears
In the official guest chamber there is a pleasant fragrance (of
    cooked foods);
Wind and rain drive across the water
But we are at ease in a cool room that overlooks the lake.

Worry and fear have now been banished
My honoured guests once more crowd my hall,
For myself I feel ashamed of living here so extravagantly
While I think of my people in want.
But let us smother these twinges of conscience [1]
And follow our natural bent.
Fresh meats are not in season
But vegetables and fruit are here to be tasted,
Deign to drink a cup of wine
While I will listen attentively to the recitation of poems.
If the spirit is happy the body feels light
I want to mount on the wings of the wind.
Soochow is the home of all the scholars.
A great wave of culture has spread itself here
How can it be said that the confines of this great state
Rest on wealth and might alone.

On meeting Fêng Chu at Chang-an

by WEI YING-WU

A STRANGER comes from the east
On his clothes the rains of Pa-ling.[2]
When we ask him wherefore he comes
He says, to buy axe to cut (firewood) from the hill.
Secretly, shyly the buds are opening,
Hither and thither the young swallows glide,
It seems only the other day that we parted
Already it is spring again ;
But our beards are whiter since our last meeting.

[1] Lit. Understanding dismiss right and wrong ; intelligence forget appearances.
[2] Szechwan.

Tarrying at Evening in the Hsü-i country

by WEI YING-WU

I FURL my sail and linger at the market town of Huai.[1]
As I anchor my boat at this lonely posting place
I hear the murmur of the wind lashing the waves
I see the daylight blotted out by night.
The peasant returns as the hills beyond the walls grow dark,
Flights of wild swans whiten the reedy islands.
In the loneliness of the night I think of the western frontier
Listening to the (monastery) bell, a sleepless stranger.

The Eastern Suburbs

by WEI YING-WU

FOR the whole year I have been cooped up in my office ;
Now outside the walls the country lies silent in the dawn.
The wind sighs quietly in the willows,
The blue hills calm my thoughts.
Amidst leafy boughs I pass the hours
Or pace the banks of a mountain stream.
A gentle rain veils the fragrant plain
Whence is the spring turtle dove calling ?
I love this peace but can seldom attain it,
Those who follow the world must hurry their footsteps.
In the end I will give up my post and here build my hut
Henceforth to imitate the example of Tao Yüan-ming.[2]

---

[1] The Huai River ran artificially into the Yangtze from 1852–1934.
[2] Ta'o Ch'ien (A.D. 365–427) who retired from official life because " he could not crook the hinges of his back for five pecks of rice." He retired to the country and occupied himself with poetry, music and the cultivation of chrysanthemums with which his name is inseparably associated.

On visiting the Priest Ch'ao's Temple Court to read the Buddhist Scriptures

by LIU TSUNG-YÜAN

I PURIFY myself with the cold water drawn from the well
With a heart at rest I shake off the dust of the world.
Leisurely I take up the palm-leaf scriptures
Walking out to the eastern lodge to read;
Though I read there is nothing in them I can read with profit,
Sordid materialism is what the world pursues.
I may search these scriptures in vain for any hope of heaven
For how can my nature attain to the perfect comprehension
    of them?
The enlightened man courts the peace of these cloistered courts
(Where) the colour of the mosses blends with the deep green of
    the bamboos.
The sun comes out through the haze
And the green pines gleam as if they were anointed with dew.
With a tranquil mind I abandon the written and spoken word
And find deep content in the joy of illumination.

Under a Frontier Post

by WANG CH'ANG-LING

THE horses are watered as I ford the autumn stream,
The river is cold, the wind cuts like a knife;
Across the flat plain the sun has not yet set;
In the dwindling light we see Lin-t'ao.[1]
In former days battles were fought here by the great wall
And valour flamed high.
Beside us things new and old mingle in a common dust
And white bones lie scattered among the wild weeds.

[1] Kansu.

A Song of Chaste Women

by MÊNG CHIAO

THE Wu-t'ung [1] trees grow old together
The mandarin duck and drake pair for life,
Even so the chaste woman prides herself on following her
    husband to the tomb
And throws away her life. [2]
I vow no waves shall ruffle the surface of my passions
Which is still as the waters of an ancient well.

Song on Climbing Yu Chou [3] Tower

by CH'ÊN TZU-ANG

LOOKING into the past I cannot see the men of old
Looking into the future I cannot see those who are to come ;
Reflecting on the immemorial and unending heaven and earth,
Alone with my grief I drop a tear.

Farewell to Ch'ên Chang-fu [4]

by LI CH'I

IN the fourth month the south wind ripens the yellow grain
The date flower has not yet fallen, the Wu-t'ung leaves are
    growing ;
In the morning we leave the blue hills
In the evening we see them in the distance.

[1] Emblematic of conjugal felicity.
[2] The practice of suttee (a widow committing suicide after the death of
her husband), although discouraged officially, often took place.
[3] Chihli. See Fletcher, *More Gems of Chinese Poetry*, p. 199.
[4] Szechwan.

Hearing a horse neigh a traveller's thoughts turn to his old home.

The Marquis Ch'ên—what a fine figure is he!

His dragon beard, his tiger eyebrows adorn a lofty forehead.

In his belly is stored the learning of a thousand volumes.

How can such as he live in retirement? [1]

At the Eastern Gate he buys wine to pledge us

His heart is light, affairs of the world seem to him like a wild goose feather.

Day has turned to night while he was drunk and asleep,

Sometimes he stares vacantly at a passing cloud high above.

The great river billows reflect the black sky,

The officer in charge of the ferry station stops his craft and cannot venture forth.

The traveller from the kingdom of Ch'ên cannot return home

The voyager from Lo-yang sighs in vain.

I have heard that in your native country you had a host of friends;

Yesterday you gave up your official position;

To-day how many of them remain?

Ode on Listening to An Wan-shan playing on the Reed Instrument

by LI CH'I

ON the southern hill a bamboo is cut to make a flageolet.

This instrument originally came from Kuei-tzŭ; [2]

But entering Chinese territory it took on a strange note.

To-day a Mongol from Liang Chou [3] makes music for me to hear

My neighbours listen; many of them sigh

Those who are exiles think of their homes and shed tears.

[1] Literally, " Lay his head on grass and flowers."
[2] A place in Sinkiang.   [3] Kansu.

The world can listen but few are able to appreciate,
(For the music conjures up) the whirlwind that comes and
    goes
(Or visions) of the dead mulberry and the old cypress soughing
    in the cold blast;
(One hears) the nine fledgelings of the phœnix cheeping
    pitifully,
The dragon booms and the tiger roars; all in chorus.
A thousand noises of nature in the music of a hundred springs
    in autumn;
Suddenly the music changes to the lament of " Yü-yang."
Desolate yellow clouds obscure the bright day.
Again the music alters and one listens to the " Willows in
    Spring."
Or " Plum Blossom in the Imperial Gardens."
On New Year's Eve the high hall is lit with bright lanterns,
A cup of good wine in my hand and this music to listen to.

A ballad of Lu Shan [1] sent to Lu Hsü-chou the Censor [2]

by LI PO

I AM no other than the wild man of Ch'u [3]
Who greeted Confucius with a mad song of derision.
In my hand I grasp a green jade staff
In the morning I leave behind the Yellow Crane pagoda;
Among the five peaks I search for the secret of immortality
Reckoning nothing of the length of the journey
For my whole life-long I have loved to wander among famous
    hills.
Lu Shan rises in splendour from the side of the Southern Dipper
A screen of nine folds of rainbow enfolds it,

[1] Near Kiukiang in Kiangsi.　　　　[2] See Obata, pp. 161–2.
[3] Chieh-yü, a drunken recluse, who stopped the chariot of Confucius
to warn him against a political career.

29

Its shadow falls on the bright lake beneath
To reflect the darkness of its black depths.
In front the " Golden Gate " lifts up its twin peaks on high
The " Silver River " drops to fall beneath the " Three Rock "
weir
Against the background of the " Censer " cataract.
Winding cliff and precipice lead up to the blue heavens
Blue green shadows and rosy mists reflect the morning sun,
Birds may not fly over the distant skies of Wu.[1]
I climb the high path and gaze at the wide prospect of heaven
and earth.
The great river flows into the distance ; it goes but does not
return.
The yellow clouds move in the wind for a thousand *li*
The white billows (of the river) encircle the hill in nine streams
as though drawn from a mountain of snow.
I love to make a ballad of Lu Shan
For Lu Shan rejoices my heart ;
In leisure I watch the " stone mirror " rock for it cleanses my
thoughts,
The paths where Hsieh (Ling-yün)[2] trod are covered by
moss.
I have eaten the drug of immortality ; my passions are spent,
I have stored up control of my mind and have thus attained the
way ;
In the distance I see the immortals in the coloured clouds ;
Grasping in their hands the hibiscus as they go to the courts of
the celestial city.

[1] Kiangsu.

[2] An eccentric scholar and poet of the fourth to fifth century who was a native of Honan. He wore clothes of an antiquated cut and roamed the hills with a company of friends. On one occasion, Giles tells us, he was mistaken for a rebel leader. He received various appointments from the early emperors of the Sung dynasty, but in 424, owing to his irritable and eccentric disposition, was banished to Kuang-tung where he mixed with disreputable characters and led a disorderly life. He was eventually beheaded.

I have an appointment with them beyond the boundaries of
    this world
Where with Lu Ao [1] I would journey to the peace of another
    world.

Dreaming of Travelling to T'ien-mu [2] and Humming a farewell Song [3]

by LI PO

THE travellers from over the seas talk of the Isles of the Blest [4]
Dim and unattainable behind their mists and waves
And difficult for the uninitiated to imagine.
The men from the south talk of the T'ien-mu mountains
Now revealed, now hidden by clouds and vapour,
Through which one may catch a glimpse.
T'ien-mu spans the length and breadth of the heavens
Its mass o'ertops the five (sacred) peaks and dwarfs the " red
    city " mountain
Before it even the mountains of T'ien-t'ai with their four
    hundred and eighty thousand feet
Seem to stagger as they lean to the south-east.
I had wanted to visit Wu [5] and Yüeh [6] in my dreams,
So one night I flew across the mirror lake under the moon
The lake moon followed my shadow to the ravines of Yen
Where the old man Hsieh [7] dwelt, whose hermitage still remains.
The shrill cries of the gibbons are wafted across the waste of
    green waters ;
With Hsieh's clogs on my feet
My body climbed on a ladder of azure cloud.

---

[1] An immortal whom Chuang-tzŭ mentions as ascending to heaven.
[2] Chekiang.   [3] See *Obata*, pp. 115-17.
[4] Ying chou, a mythical fairy island which the Japanese have identified
with Japan.
[5] Kiangsu.   [6] Chekiang.   [7] Hsieh Ling-yün.

From half-way up the cliff I saw the sun rising from the sea
In the empty heavens I heard the heavenly chicken crow,[1]
By a thousand peaks and ten thousand precipices there was no
    certain road.
Bewitched by the flowers I rested against a rock
Suddenly it became dark ;
Bears roared and the dragons bellowed ; mountain torrents
    thundered the echoes,
I trembled among deep forests and shuddered from the terraced
    peaks,
Dark, dark, the lowering clouds that threatened rain
Rough and storm-tossed the waters from which the mists are
    born,
The thunder rolled and the lightning flashed
Hills and ridges burst asunder,
The stone gates of the heavenly mansions broke apart,
A crashing noise and chasms gape in the darkness
Revealing dim abyss of bottomless depth.
The brightness of sun and moon shone on the gold and silver
    terraces
The rainbow clouds their garments, the wind their steeds,
The spirits of the clouds dropped tumultuously to the earth
    below,
Tigers were their lute-players, the phœnix gambled round their
    chariots ;
Before them the Hsien were marshalled like stalks of hemp.
Suddenly my unconscious mind is jolted and my conscious
    mind comes to life,
I start and sit up with a long sigh
Alas ! I awoke to my pillow and bed ; gone were the mists
    and clouds (that bore me).
In this world happiness is always like this
All things pass like the east flowing water.

[1] A legendary fowl with three legs which lived in the sun. The cock
in any form is an embodiment of the *yang* element which represents the
warmth and life of the universe.

The parting guest is sped, when shall we meet again?
Let me loose a white deer to roam among the dark ravines
So that as it starts forth I may mount on its back to visit famous
hills.
How can I bend the bow and crook the back to the rich and
mighty
And so stifle my own soul?

At Hsüan Chou [1] in the Hsieh T'iao Pavilion Entertaining the Secretary Shu Yün at a parting banquet

by LI PO

ALAS! You desert me and go, the pleasures of yesterday
cannot be stayed
While to-day racks me with all its sorrows.
The distant winds that blow for over a thousand li speed the
autumn geese,
In face of this let us tipple in the high pavilion.
Your literary style uniting P'êng-lai [2] form with Chien-an [2]
vigour
With an admixture of the dainty and sweep of the little Hsieh [3]
With untrammelled zest and the strong wings of fancy
Would soar to the azure heaven and gaze at the bright moon.
Cut water with a knife and the water will still flow on,
Fill a cup to banish sorrow, the sorrow but grows.
Life is never as a man would have it;
To-morrow with loose locks I shall wander away in a fragile
barque

[1] Anhui.   [2] Styles of Chinese calligraphy.
[3] Probably Hsieh T'iao, a native of Yang-hsia who flourished in the
fifth century. A distinguished poet, upon whose works Shên Yo is said
to have exclaimed, "For two hundred years we have not had poetry like
this." Possibly Hsieh Hui-lien, younger brother of the famous fifth-
century scholar Hsieh Ling-yün.

Saying Farewell to General Fêng as he rides his Horses across the River and sets forth to lead his Troops on a Western Campaign

by TS'ÊN TS'AN

Do you not see where they ride their horses across the river
And away to the lake of snow ?
The flat sands stretch away on every side an endless yellow
    prospect merging with the sky ;
Around Lun-t'ai [1] in the ninth moon the wind rages at
    night,
The whole river (is full) of fragments of boulders as big as a
    peck measure
When the wind blows the whole river-bed is full of tumbling
    rocks.
The Hsiung-nu [2] pastures are yellow, but their horses are fat.
To the west of the Gold Hill one sees thin clouds of dust ;
The Chinese General leads his troops to the west
The commander cannot remove his armour all night long,
In the middle of the night the troops take the road, their weapons
    clanking at their sides.
The wind is as a knife as it cuts the face,
The snow lies on the horses' hides, their sweat rises like steam
The five flower [3] (trappings) and the coin metalwork are
    incrusted with icicles.
As you in your tent draft despatches the ink on the slab is
    frozen.
But the barbarian cavalry hear of your coming and fear fills
    their minds,
Can it be that their dirks dare not come to grips ?
The (rest) of the army waits at the western gate for the news of
    your victory.

[1] Manchuria.   [2] Mongol tribe.
[3] Possibly a reference to a five-flower horse, i.e. a piebald.

The white Snow Song of Farewell to the Military Secretary Wu returning Home

by TS'ÊN TS'AN

THE wind rolls up from the north,
The ground is white and the reeds break (beneath the weight of
    snow)
In the eighth month the Tartar heaven is filled with flying snow.
Suddenly as if in a night a breath of spring had blown
A thousand, ten thousand trees (under their mantle of snow)
    are white as pear blossom ;
(The wind) pierces the bead curtains and damps the gauze
    hangings,
The fox skin robes are not warm enough, the embroidered
    quilt is thin.
The General's horn bows cannot be stretched
The town guard feel their suits of mail strike chill but still they
    don them ;
The cliffs of the northern seas are covered with ice for their
    whole length,
The lowering clouds dismal and motionless hang for a thousand
    li.
The General offers wine and drinks to the parting guest,
The Tartar violin, the guitar and the Ch'iang fife entertain
    them.
Flake upon flake of the evening snow pile up before the yamen [1]
    gate,
The wind tears at the red flag but it is frozen and will not
    unfurl,
From the east gate of Lun-t'ai [2] city I speed you on your way.
As you go the snow deepens on the road to T'ien Shan, [3]
The curve of the hill and turn in the road hide you
No trace remains but the footprints of the horses' hoofs upon
    the snow.

[1] The official residence of the Governor or Viceroy, or the magistrate.
[2] Manchuria.   [3] Turkestan.

35

Sending a letter to Mr. Han, the Censor

by TU FU

TO-DAY I was not happy, but I thought of Yo Chou,[1]
My body wished to spread its wings and fly, but sickness kept
    me to my bed.
I thought of you with all the charm [2] of youth cut off from me
    by the autumn waters [3]
Washing your feet in the Tung-t'ing Lake,[4]
And gazing over the eight quarters of the compass.
A Wild swan flew into the distance white as the sun or
    moon.
The leaves of the green maple turn red,
The sky is like to drop hoar frost,
In the Jade Palace a crowd of immortals gather round the Great
    Bear,
Some astride kylins, others phœnixes :
Hibiscus banners merge into the mists,
The morning shadows are (reflected) upside down on the sur-
    face of the lake and ruffle the faces of Hsiao and Hsiang.[5]
In the starry palace of the immortals the divine beings are drunk
    with nectar,
One is missing from the ranks of their winged attendants ;
It is as if I hear again Ch'ih-sung Tzŭ [6] of old
Or do I see Chang Liang [6] of Han ? In the Han dynasty
Of old he (Chang Liang) served Liu in the founding of Ch'ang-an.

[1] Kuang-ling in Hupei.
[2] The phrase used here is usually restricted to women. His friend seems
to have had an almost girlish charm quite incongruous with his position
as censor. For similar use of the term applied to a male see *Odes*, Pt. I,
Book III, Ode 14, S. 4.
[3] i.e. in disgrace at Court.   [4] Between Hunan and Hupei.
[5] Two rivers in Hunan.
[6] Chang Liang was a statesman who helped to found the Han dynasty.
After the Emperor Kao Tsu had succeeded in uniting China, he (Chang
Liang) became like his tutor Ch'ih-sung Tzŭ (the Wizard of the Red
Pine) a Taoist recluse.

His political schemes never came to grief but his spirit was
    afflicted.
Why concern oneself with the rise and fall of states ?
What is the stench of flesh-meats compared with a diet of
    liquidambar ? [1]
In the south Ssŭ-ma T'an [2] was kept lingering and frustrated,
    that is an old theme for sorrow ;
But the South Pole Star brings long life and prosperity.
How is it that you are separated by the autumn waters [3]
How can we get you back to Court ?

Drunken Song on the Stone Fish Pond

by YÜAN CHIEH

(I HAVE used grain from the public fields to distil wine. After
my office hours I take wine to the side of the lake. Then I
invite my friends for a drinking bout. They sit and tipple on
the shores of the lake and pledge the fish with wine. Wine
boats ply to and fro to supply them as they sit scattered about.
We seem to be drinking on the Pa islet surrounded by the
Tung-t'ing Lake. The wine boats float about, the ripples on
the water come and go. So I make this song and chant it so
as to prolong it.)

The stone fish lake is a miniature Tung-t'ing ;
In summer the water is like to overflow and the Chün Hill
    (stands out) dark blue.
The hill is a goblet,
The water a pool (of wine) ;
We tipplers scattered on all sides
Sit on the rocky island.

[1] From the resin of this tree the Taoists brew an elixir of life.
[2] Son of the Emperor K'ang Ti and fifth sovereign of the Eastern Chin.
[3] i.e. in disgrace.

A steady wind blows throughout the day
Ruffling the lake into ripples
But does not deter the men from bringing up the wine boats.
I grasp a long gourd calabash sitting on the islet of Pa.[1]
On the hill we drink scattered in all quarters,
So we drive away melancholy.

The Hill Rocks

by HAN YÜ

THE mountain boulders reveal the faint impression of a dangerous
    and rugged path;
In the yellow dusk I come on a monastery,
The bats wheel around me
As I sit on the steps of the main hall.
The freshly fallen rain has just ceased
The leaves of the plantain are now fully spread,
The gardenia buds are bursting.
The monk tells me the Buddhist frescoes are good;
He brings a torch to light them for me,
But what is seen is faint.
He spreads out the bed and stakes down the mat,
He sets out soup and rice, coarse yet ample enough to satisfy
    my hunger.
The night is dark and I rest in peace,
All the insects go to rest;
A clear moon rises above the mountain and shines in through
    the door.
At earliest dawn under bright heavens I go on my way alone,
I cannot see my path (because it is so early)
Now losing it, now striking it again,
Stumbling and recovering, lost in mist and haze.
The hills are bathed in red, the mountain streams show blue;
Numerous (streams) sparkle and meander on their way;

[1] Hunan.

38

From time to time I see pine and oak ten spans round,
When my path crosses a stream I wade over the stones with
bare feet ;
The sound of the water tinkles in my ears,
The wind blows through my clothes,
If only life were always like this—how happy man might be !
Why must the affairs of men bind him as it were with bit and
bridle ?
I would say to my friends
How can I not wish to grow old here and why should I return
home ?

*On the 15th evening of the 8th month presented to Chang the
Keeper of the Records (in a provincial yamen)*

by HAN YÜ

DELICATE clouds roll up and disappear
The sky is so bright that you cannot see the Milky Way ;
A pure wind blows through the empty heavens,
The rays of the moon are scattered o'er the waves ;
Murmur and shadow fade away [1] on quiet sands and still waters.
One cup of wine we will drink together
Then you shall sing a song ;
The lilt of your song is melancholy and the phrases full of bitter
thoughts,
One cannot listen to the end before the tears fall like rain.
The Tung-t'ing (lake) stretches away to the sky,
The Chiu-i [2] mountain is high ;
Crocodiles and dragons come and go, apes and vampires cry,
Nine out of ten die before reaching this official post.[3]

[1] Literally all-consummate, perfect, transcendent.   [2] In Hunan.
[3] The author and his friend had been exiled to the south.   Then came
a general amnesty and they were allowed to return, but owing to intrigues
instead of getting complete reinstatement they were given minor posts,
of which he goes on to complain.

In squalid dark houses we hide ourselves,
When we left our beds we were frightened of snakes,
When we eat we were frightened of poison ;
The summer air from the sea was damp and pestiferous,
The smells rank and rancid.
But there came a day when before the yamen they beat the big
    drum ;
A new emperor had succeeded to the sacred line
And had elevated loyal servants.
An amnesty travels a thousand miles in a single day ;
Those under sentence of death need not die,
The exiled ones were recalled,
The banished could return home.
All stains and impurities were to be things of the past
The new emperor opens a bright new page,
Our senior officials suggest our names, his seniors suppress
    them ;
Frustrated, what is left for us but to move to yet more barbaric
    surroundings ? [1]
Our present post is small and not to be spoken of,
How can we avoid being trampled and buffeted as we lie in the
    dust ?
Most of our contemporaries follow the road back to official
    success,
But that road is dark and dangerous and hard to attain.
Your song—come stop it,
Listen to my song.
My sentiments are very [2] different from yours,
Of all the full moons in the year to-night's is the brightest.
Man from birth is governed by fate, and nothing else,
If you have wine and do not drink it
Will to-morrow be any the better ?

[1] ? to the wilds of Ch'u.
[2] One reading has " not different from yours."

The Stone Drum Song [1]

by HAN YÜ

MR. CHANG in his hand grasps the stone drum rubbing
He encourages me to compose a stone drum song.
The bard of Shao Ling [2] is no more
The banished angel is dead ; [3]
My talents are scanty, how can I deal with such a theme !
When the administration of Chou decayed and the empire was
    in turmoil,
Then the Emperor Hsuan [4] rose in his might and brandished his
    celestial spear.

---

[2] The poet Tu Fu.   [3] The poet Li Po.

[1] and [4] From S. W. Bushell, *Chinese Art*, Vol. 1, 1904, pp. 32 etc. :

The most cherished relics of the Chou dynasty are ten stone drums, now installed in the two side halls of the principal gateway of the Confucian Temple at Peking, where they were placed in the year 1307 by Kuo Shou-ching, the famous minister and astronomer of the reigns of Kublai Khan and his successor. They are really mountain boulders roughly chiselled into the shape of drums, about three feet high, the form of which may be seen in Fig. 6, reproduced from a photograph taken in Peking by Mr. J. Thomson, the learned photographer now attached to the Royal Geographical Society. The picture shows how the drum on the right has been truncated and scooped out to make a mortar for pounding grain, involving the loss of nearly half of its inscription, an allusion to which occurs in the well-known verses by the celebrated poet Han Yü, written in 812, which have been engraved on a marble stele erected in the Confucian Temple by the Emperor Ch'ien Lung, accompanied by a laudatory ode of his own composition.

The stone drums were discovered in the early part of the seventh century, lying half-buried in the ground in the vicinity of Fêng-hsiang Fu in the province of Shensi, on the south of the hills called Ch'i Shan, from which the district city of Ch'i-shan Hsien takes its name. T'ai Wang, an ancestor of the Chou, moved to this locality in the year 1325 B.C., and it continued to be the capital of the Chou State till the time of Wên Wang, who is said to have made the hunting park on the south of Mount Ch'i, surrounded by a wall seventy *li* square, which is supposed to have been the " Great Park " of our inscription (Fig. 7). The drums were set up in the Confucian Temple of Fêng-hsiang Fu about A.D. 820. When the Sung emperor fled from the Kitan Tartars to the province of

Wide were flung the doors of the " bright hall " to receive
    Court congratulations,
Marquises (came) with their pendent swords jangling as they
    rattled against each other,
They hunted on the southern slopes of Mount Ch'i [1]
The galloping of their horses was a fine sight ;

Honan and founded a new capital there, a hall was specially built in the
new grand palace, finished in 1119, for the exhibition of the drums, an
edict having been issued that the inscriptions should be filled in with gold,
to betoken their value, and, at the same time, to prevent their further
injury by the hammer in taking rubbings. But they rested here a few
years only, for the Juchen Tartars sacked the city in 1126, dug out the
gold inlay, and carried off the drums to their own central capital, the
modern Peking.

The inscriptions on the stone drums comprise a series of ten odes, a
complete one being cut on each drum, composed in rhyming stanzas of
irregular verse, in the style of the odes of the early Chou period which
are preserved in the *Shih Ching*, the canonical *Book of Odes* compiled by
Confucius. They celebrate an imperial hunting and fishing expedition
in the country where the drums were found, and relate how the roads
had been levelled and the river courses cleared for a grand battue carried
out by troops of warriors marshalled under the command of the feudal
princes. The cyclical number of the *day* is given in one line, but there
is nothing to indicate the year, and Chinese authorities unfortunately
differ as to their probable date. It must, at any rate, be before 770 B.C.,
when we have seen that the capital of the Chou was moved eastwards
to Loyang, and their ancestral territory ceded to the rising State of Ch'in,
which was destined eventually to supplant them. The older authorities
generally referred the inscriptions, on literary grounds chiefly, to the
reign of Hsüan Wang (827–782 B.C.), but several competent scholars of
more recent date attribute them to Ch'êng Wang (1115–1079 B.C.), on
grounds which seem to me to be well founded. Both the *Bamboo Books*
and the *Annals of Lu* mention a grand hunting expedition to the south of
Mount Ch'i in the spring of the sixth year of Ch'êng Wang, on his return
from a military expedition to the Huai river in the east, and drums are
reasonably supposed to have been inscribed on this occasion. The archaic
character of the script and its analogies with inscriptions of the time on
bronze vessels newly unearthed, tend to strengthen the argument, although
it is not universally accepted. Waiving the question of their exact date, the
stone drums may be accepted as certainly early relics of the Chou dynasty.

[1] Shensi.

For ten thousand miles (the corpses) of birds and animals were
  strewn and scattered.
He cut and chiselled (these drums) to record his achievement
  for the information of ages to come;
To chisel the stone to make the drums they destroyed a jutting
  crag.
The officials he employed were all first-class craftsmen
He selected them and bade them compose the text and engrave
  it:
But the stones were left exposed on the hill-side.
The rain has soaked them, the sun has scorched them, forest
  fires have burnt them,
But the fairy spirits have guarded them and cherished them.
From where, Mr. Chang, I wonder did you get this rubbing?
Not a hair's breadth differing from the original, without the
  least error
The style is severe, the meaning secret and hard to understand;
The style of the characters is not the " li "[1] or the tadpole [1]
Years have passed and some strokes must be missing;
The strokes are like sharp swords that cut in twain living dragons
  and lizards,
The *luan* [2] soar and the phœnix wheel, a crowd of immortals
  beneath them;
The coral and jade trees entwine their branches interlocked,
Golden cords and iron ropes twist and interlock
(Elusive as) the ancient tripod that leapt into the waters,
Or a shuttle rising to heaven in the form of a dragon.
The meagre scholars (of that day) wrote but forgot to mention
  them,
Therefore the Two Ya [3] were constricted and not entirely
  complete.

---

[1] Two different styles of script.   [2] A green phœnix.
[3] i.e. the drum inscription ought to have been included in the material
from which Confucius drew the *Shih Ching*, but the compilers had not
enough scholarship so the *Shih Ching* suffered.   The two Ya are sections
of the *Shih Ching*.

Confucius on his journey to the west did not reach Ch'in,[1]
So his anthology as it were included the stars but omitted the sun and moon.
Alas ! I luckless who love ancient things was born too late
And when I think of this my tears flow down like torrents ;
I remember when I was first appointed Doctor in the Academy
In the first year of Yüan-ho.[2]
An old friend who was a soldier in the garrison of the right
Went into the matter for me and excavated round the site where the drums lay buried.
I washed my hat and myself with reverent ceremony before reporting to my chief saying
" How many precious things like these have been preserved ?
They ought to be wrapped in felt and covered in matting and then could be removed speedily ;
These ten drums could be carried easily on the backs of a few camels.
My proposal is they should be (exhibited) in the Great Temple like the Kao incense tripod,
But their glory and value exceed the latter by more than a hundredfold ;
Or if his holy Majesty permits let them be put in the academy
Where scholars would be able to expound and explain them by intensive research
(Just as in the olden days) when the Classics (were engraved in stone) and set up outside the Hung-tu.
Then (the carriages) would fill the street, and while men sat and looked the whole country would come hastening like waves of the sea.
Scoop out the lichen and scrape the moss to expose the characters knots and horns,
Place them in precise arrangement, evenly and without crookedness
(Build) a massive pavilion with deep eaves to cover it
That will last for long periods and defy time."

[1] i.e. Shensi. He had no chance of seeing the originals.   [2] A.D. 806.

44

But the great officials of court had grown slack in their duties

How could they be interested or moved? for choice they
vacillate and hesitate;

So the shepherd boy strikes fire on the drums and the cattle
sharpen their horns on them,

Who else is there to caress or care for them?

Just now all is peaceful and there are no troubles,

Authority is entrusted to men of learning

Men honour Confucius and Mencius:

But how can I get this matter put down for fuller considera-
tion? [1]

I wish I could borrow the mouth of an orator that flowed like
a waterfall.

The song of the stone drums finishes here,

But alas! My thoughts are all fruitless and vain

(Since I made the above recommendation without success)

Suns have waxed and moons waned, and soon they will be
buried and disappear.

For six years I have gazed to the west [2] in vain making my
plaint.

Wang Hsi-chih's carved script was the cause of adoration and
pleasure, [3]

Yet some papers of them could be exchanged for a few white
geese. [4]

Since Chou there have been eight dynasties [5] fraught with
strife, which only now has ceased,

Yet no one collects or cares for these drums.

What is the reason for it?

[1] See Mencius V, Pt. 2, Chap. 8, S. 2.

[2] Because they were found in Shensi.

[3] His calligraphy was much prized, yet this ancient script, which ought
to be even more highly valued, is left unheeded.

[4] Wang Hsi-chih made a copy of the *Tao-tê Ching* for a Taoist priest
in return for a flock of geese.

[5] Ch'in, Han, Chin, Sung, Ch'i, Liang, Ch'ên, Sui.

The Poem of the Guitar [1]

by PO CHÜ-I

(IN the tenth year of Yüan-ho [2] I was banished and sent to be
an assistant official in Kiukiang. In the autumn of the next
year I was seeing off a friend at the mouth of the P'ên-p'u [3]
when I heard at midnight from a neighbouring boat a guitar
played after the manner of the capital. On asking I found the
player was a courtezan from Chang-an and had learnt the guitar
there. When she grew old and her beauty faded she had been
married to a merchant. I invited her to our boat to drink wine
and to play us a few stanzas. When her tunes were ended, she
told us sadly of the heyday of her youth. Now she was deserted
and melancholy and a wanderer. Since I had left the capital
two years before I had been not unhappy but that evening the
girl's playing awoke sad thoughts, and because of it I wrote this
long poem, six hundred and twelve characters, and called it the
" Poem of the Guitar.")

One night at Hsün-yang [4] at the head of the Yangtze River
    I sped the parting guest,
The maple leaves and flowering rushes rustled in the autumn,
    (breeze)
The host remounted his horse, the guest entered the boat;
Raising our wine cups we were about to drink but we missed
    the strains of music.
Drunk we were not completely happy, for the farewell weighed
    on our minds.
When the moment of parting came, far far the river stretched
    swallowing the moon :
Suddenly we heard on the water the sound of a guitar
The host forgot to dismount, the guest did not set out ;
Seeking the voice we asked in hushed tones who the player
    might be ?

[1] Translated Giles, *Chinese Literature*, pp. 165–7.   [2] 815.
[3] Kiukiang, Kiangsi.   [4] Kiukiang.

The guitar's strains ceased and we were discreetly answered:
We moved our boat nearer and requested the player to join us,
The wine is replenished, the lamp was relit and the feast re-opened;
After a thousand requests and ten thousand entreaties she consented to appear.
Still clasping her guitar so as to half hide her face
Grasping the shaft she struck two or three notes,
Before she has completed the prelude she betrayed her emotion.
The strings were struck and muted and their notes produced her thoughts
As if she was telling how her whole life was unhappy.
She lowered her eyebrows, she let her hands stray over the chords as she played,
She spoke with a full heart not hiding her feelings.
Lightly she plucked the strings and slowly she tuned (and twisted the pegs)
She caressed and picked out (the notes).
Then she began with the " Song of the Rainbow Skirt and the Feathered Jacket ";
Afterwards with the " Six young girls."
The bass strings crashed like torrential rains,
The trebles murmured like secret whispers
Now loud now soft together
As big pearls and little pearls are dropped into a jade bowl,
Or as the liquid call of the oriole gliding beneath flowering (trees).
(We heard) the dark pent up stream flow down to the rapids
And now like a spring gripped by frost
The strings were brought to a standstill and abruptly the notes died away;
In the sadness and melancholy of another my secret grief made itself known,[1]

[1] Alternative translation, " but dying gives birth to sorrow and hidden grief."

And at that moment silence was more poignant even than music ;
(As she continued) the silver bowl was suddenly broken, the water gushed away,
Armoured riders rushed out, knives and spears clashed together ;
The tune finished she put aside (her lute) but she struck once just at the last
Four strings sounded together like ripping silk.
The east boat and west boat were silent without a word,
Only visible was the heart of the river white in the autumn moon.
Murmuring to herself she tucked the plectrum into the middle of the strings,
Arranging and adjusting her dress she resumed a modest pose.
In her own words she tells us she was originally a city girl
Her home was at the foot of the Hsia-ma Ling.
At the age of thirteen she mastered the P'i-p'a [1] completely.
Her name in the teaching school ranked among the first class ;
Her apprenticeship over she became one of the experts,[2]
Dressed in her best she aroused jealousy of even Ch'iu Niang.[3]
The smart young dogs of Wu-ling [4] vied with each other to fee her [5]
For one tune one did not know how much red silk.
Inlaid pins and silver combs were broken and shattered in fragments,
Skirts of blood-red silk were stained with wine.
This year happy and laughing and again next,
The spring breeze the autumn moon has passed without heeding.
Her younger brother went off to the wars,
Her mother died
Evenings came and went as her beauty faded.

[1] Guitar.
[2] After hearing her song the maestro himself had been impressed by her talent.
[3] A famous T'ang beauty.   [4] Hunan.
[5] Ch'an t'ou (bandaged heads) was money given to a singing girl.

Her front door became cold and neglected,
The horse-chaises were few.
When she has withered she marries a merchant—
A merchant who thinks only of his profits and lightly of leaving
  her.
Last month he went off to Fou Liang [1] to buy tea
When he had gone she came to the mouth of the river in her
  empty boat,
Above her boat the bright moon, (below) the winter waters
  of the river.
In the dark night suddenly she dreams of her youthful years,
In her dream she weeps and the rouge on her face comes off
  with her tears and stains the railings red.
When I heard the P'i-p'a already I was reduced to sobs and sighs
  when I heard her story I was sadder still :
Together we shared the same sorrow for we were cold and
  neglected people,
Though we met for the first time what did it matter we had
  not met before ?
Last year I quitted the Imperial capital
Banished I lay sick at Hsün-yang.
Hsün-yang is very secluded ; there is no music
For a whole year I had not heard either string or bamboo
  instruments.
I live by the river near P'ên Pu city, the ground is low and damp,
Yellow reeds and bitter bamboos surround my house ;
What do I hear between dusk and dawn
But the cries of the nightjars and the howls of the gibbon ?
In spring when flowers bloom of a morning by the river or on
  a moonlight night in autumn
I raise my cup constantly and drain it all alone.
And although there are mountain songs and village flutes,
Yet they are horrid and unharmonious, grating and tuneless
  and hard to listen to :
This night I had heard the notes of a professional

[1] Kiangsi.

It was like listening to fairy music and my ears for a while were
   open.
Don't refuse, (I said) sit down again and play one more tune
While I put your story on paper as the song of the lute.
Moved by my words she who had been standing sat down and
   grasping her lute tight broke into a rapid song
In melancholy strains not like her former music.
The notes touched the whole audience
And all of us hearing her again, with difficulty kept back our
   tears.
Among those who sat there, who had to suppress most?
The Sub-prefect of Chiang Chou [1] whose dark blue dress was
   wet.

The Stone Inscription of Han Yü

by LI SHANG-YIN

IN the Yüan-ho [2] period Hsien Tsung had the endowments of
   a divine warrior:
What a man he was. Huang Ti [3] and Fu Hsi [4] (can only be
   compared with him).
He swore he would wipe out the disgrace of his ancestors
Sitting in his palace of justice he gave audience to the four
   barbarians from all the four quarters.
To the west of the Huai River there had been brigands for fifty
   years

[1] i.e. the poet himself.
[2] A.D. 805–20 Hsien Tsung reigned from 805–20.
[3] The Yellow Emperor, one of the most famous of China's legendary
rulers. Said to have reigned 2698–2598 B.C. and to be the inventor of
wheeled vehicles, pottery, armour and ships.
[4] The first of the five emperors of the legendary period (said to have
reigned 2953–2838 B.C.). He taught people to handle fish and keep
cattle and make musical instruments; cook and keep a calendar. From
the markings on the back of a tortoise he is said to have constructed the
Eight Diagrams from which was developed the whole philosophy
embodied in the Book of Changes.

Boundary wolves had bred lynxes, and lynxes, bears.

When the rebels were not in possession of the hills and villages
they were in possession of the plains;

Their long spears and sharp lances, they brandished every day.

The Emperor procured a wise minister whose name was Tu

The brigands tried to assassinate him, but he did not die for the
heavens supported him;

From his girdle hung his seals of office and he was made Com-
mander-in-Chief.

(In those days) a dark wind blew grimly upon the imperial
banners.

The Generals Su, Wu, Ku and T'ung were made his teeth and
claws;

Secretaries with their pens were in his train,

Field officers also with skill (to plan) and bravery (to perform);

One hundred and forty thousand soldiers like tigers and leopards

They entered Ts'ai and tied up the rebel chief and later exhibited
him at the imperial ancestral temple.

Their merit was incomparable; the imperial bounty was
limitless

The Emperor said " You, Tu, are meritorious beyond all and
that follower of yours, Yü, ought to make a record of
events.

Yü made obeisance, bowed his head and danced to show his
gratification, (and said)—

' In engraving on metal and stone and in carving and painting
your servant is proficient;

From of old the title of great calligraphist has not been bestowed
by virtue of official position

And those who were upright from of old never refused (to use
the pen)." [1]

When he had finished speaking the Imperial head was frequently
nodded in agreement,

He went back and retired to sit in a small room to purify himself

Then moistening and drying his long brushes,

[1] See *Analects*, XV, 35.

How he dripped and splashed !

In blobs and strokes (he drew) characters in the style of the
    canon of Yao and the canon of Shun ; [1]

Then he erased and altered, following the style of the " Pure
    Temple," [2]

And of the " Light of the People." [3]

When the essay was complete he wrote it on paper in the
    cursive style ;

Early in the morning he again bowed and spread it on the purple
    terrace.

He spoke out " I your subject greatly daring submit this

The song of your sacred merits, please have it written on stone "

The tablet was thirty feet high and the characters as big as ladles

It was set on the back of a spiritual tortoise [4] round which the
    dragons coiled ;

It was full of strange phraseology and obscure references that
    few could understand.

(But) the author was slandered to the Emperor on the ground
    that he was biased.

With ropes one hundred feet long they pulled down the table

With coarse granite and big rocks they defaced and rubbed it

Yet the text had a lively vitality

And before it was defaced it had already impressed itself on the
    minds of men.

Like the T'ang tub and K'ung tripod its history has been recorded

To-day these objects do not exist but their inscriptions have
    been preserved.

Alas ! for the wise king and the sage minister ;

Yet these two have shared their own fame and glory with the
    ebb and flow of the country's prosperity. [5]

[1] *Shu Ching.*   [2] *Shih Ching.*   [3] *Shi Ching,* III, 2, S. 1.

[4] Stone tortoises are invariably used to support stelæ in North China
Pan ku, who dreated the world, was supposed to set it on the back of
tortoise.

[5] Meaning that in the case of the T'ang tub and K'ung tripod a sage
king and a sage minister had left a glorious record to posterity, but that
in the case of Han Yü his effort was doomed to perish.

et if this tablet's contents do not pass down to posterity
am eager with the help of two or three like-minded with
   myself to reach up and rescue the inscriptions from oblivion.
would wish to write ten thousand copies and to recite it ten
   thousand times,
ntil the corners of my mouth dripped with saliva
nd my right wrist was callous,
nd to hand it down for seventy-two generations.
would have it used at the *fêng shan* sacrifice as a jade strip or
   be laid in the foundations of the Bright Hall.

An ancient Marching Song
by LI CH'I (*written to music*)

the white dawn we climb the hill ; distant beacon fires burn.
the deepening dusk we water our horses beside the Chiao
   river.
dles and dippers clash about the marching host,
arkness veils the wind-blown sand.
he princess's guitar speaks endlessly of her ancient sorrows -
amping in empty spaces ten thousand miles distant from any
   city wall ;
ain and snowflake upon flake cover the great Gobi desert,
he Tartar wild geese bay sadly night after night as they wing
   their way overhead.
he tears of the Tartar horsemen fall drop by drop.
e hear the Jade Gate Pass is still blocked by the foe ;
uty requires us to take our lives in our hands and draw our
   frail chariots home,[2]

[1] A reference to the state marriage of Wang Chao-chün, a Chinese
incess of the court of the Emperor Yüan, to a Tartar prince, an
isode of the Han dynasty. The lady died after she reached her destina-
n but the songs of misery she composed in her exile were supposed to
ger round the frontiers she crossed to meet her Tartar husband.
[2] The troops are trying to get back to China but the Huns hold the
sses.

Fighting from year to year our bones litter the wastes beyond
All this was done that grapes may enter China.[1]

The Song of the Girl of Lo-yang

by WANG WEI

THE girl of Lo-yang [2] lives opposite ; she looks as if she may
    fifteen years old.
Her lover sits on a piebald horse with a jade bridle,
Her serving girls serve her with minced carp on a gold plate
Her painted pavilions and crimson halls repeat themselves o
    upon another,
Red peach and green willow hang down towards the eave
When she leaves her silken curtains she is ushered forth in
    seven-scented litter,
When she comes home to her nine flowered screens she
    welcomed by jewelled fans.
(Her lord) is a daring young man, rich and noble and in t
    spring of his youth,
His airs and graces are even more proud and lavish than tho
    of Chi-lun.[3]
Out of his infatuation he covers her with green jade [4] and o
    of his love for her she is taught to dance,
Nor does he begrudge coral and gives it away to anyone.
In the spring window at dawn the nine subtle flames a
    extinguished,[5]
And (the smoke of their extinction) floats down in the wind
    flowery wisps.

[1] The grape is supposed to have been introduced from the west in
form of tribute.

[2] In Honan, a former capital.

[3] A native of Shantung renowned for extravagance who lived in
Chin dynasty. He is credited with using wax for firewood.

[4] Pi Yü may be the name of his mistress.

[5] The reference is to a kind of lamp with nine small wicks.

When the entertainment is over there is no time to rehearse
    songs
But only to powder (the face) ;
Fragrant and perfumed she sits (waiting for her guest).
In the town her companions form a brilliant escort.
Daily and nightly she frequents the Chao's and the Li's,[1]
She even feels pity for the beauty of Yüeh [2] on the score
That as she was once poor and humble she did her own washing.

The Snare of Beauty [3]

by TU FU

On the third day of the third month [4] as the weather was
    perfect
By the side of the water of Ch'ang-an walked many beautiful
    women ;
Their voluptuous poise betokened their unconscious thoughts,
    yet they were pure and true.
Their skins were glossy and smooth, bones and flesh evenly
    balanced,
The embroidered gauze of their clothes reflected the glow of a
    late spring day
Stamped with gold peacocks and silver unicorns.
What did they have on their heads ?
Kingfisher-blue head-dresses of leaves hanging down from the
    hair at each side.
What do you see on their backs ?
Trains from the waist stitched with pearls fitting perfectly to
    the body.

[1] i.e. two rich and noble families of the Han dynasty, who maintained
many dancing girls and gay company.

[2] She is so proud that she affects sorrow for Hsi-shih the famous beauty,
who, because of her beauty, was lifted from the laundry to the palace.

[3] A description of the Court of Ming Huang and the ladies that surrounded Yang Kuei-fei.

[4] This was a spring Court festival of the time of Ming Huang.

In their midst the ladies of the " clouded tent "[1] and the
" pepper room,"[1]
On whom His Majesty has bestowed the great titles of " Kuo
Kuo "[2] and " Ch'in Kuo."[2]
For their delight the purple camel hump is brought from its
blue jade cauldron
And crystal plates bear in the delicate carp.
Rhinoceros-horn chopsticks are plied till they are exhausted and
they can be tempted no further,[3]
And the green phœnix knife is poised a long time over delicious
morsels,
When suddenly through the yellow door fly the imperial
horses so fast that they do not stir the dust
Bringing from the imperial kitchens the eight famous dainties
in one continuous stream.
(To-day) flute and drum sound sadly stirring the ghosts,
(Yesterday) the guests crowded the assembly, all were of high
rank.
At length came a saddled horse ; with what state His Majesty
rides !
At the pavilion, dismounting from his horse, he sinks upon the
embroidered pillows.
(To-day) the catkins of the willow drop like snow upon the
white duckweed.[4]
The green birds fly away bearing the red cloth.[5]
Play with fire and you have burnt fingers, and this is calculated
to destroy relationships

[1] Parts of the palace reserved for imperial concubines and for eunuchs.
Perhaps " in their midst ladies of the Pepper Room with its cloud-
embroidered curtains."

[2] Title bestowed upon the two sisters of Yang Kuei-fei.

[3] The meaning is that these people were so spoilt with luxurious living
that even the choicest food makes no appeal.

[4] Willow is here a play on the name of Yang and the duckweed is
symbol of mourning, i.e. to-day the Emperor honours the death of
Yang Kuei-fei.

[5] ? happiness departs.

Oh why were you not more wary to heed the prime minister[1]
and his angry looks ?

Sacrificing to Confucius when passing through Lu and pitying him by the EMPEROR HSÜAN TSUNG.[2]

To think, my master, you wandered about derelict through
a whole age,[3]
Yet this place is still the District City of Tsou.[4]
Though your home was made the palace of the King of Lu[5]
The pitying phœnix lamented your frustration ;
When you grieved for the unicorn you were repining at the
failure of your own teaching.
When I look now at the sacrifice between the two pillars
Can it be that ill-omened sacrifice you dreamed of long ago ?[6]

An Occasional Poem[7]

by SHÊN CH'ÜAN-CH'I

I HAVE heard it said that at the frontier defences of Huang-
lung[8]
Year after year there is no soldier's leave ;
Yet the (self-same) moon that shines on our women's apartments

[1] Yang Kuo-chung, cousin of Yang Kuei-fei, who warned Ming
Huang of the coming rebellion of An Lu-shan.
[2] This poem is loaded with classical allusions and quotations and is just
an exhibition of virtuosity.
[3] See *Analects*, XIV, 34.   [4] i.e. still your birth-place.
[5] During the Han dynasty the King of Lu, on breaking down the walls
of his palace, found ancient writings and recognizing it as former abode of
Confucius, made it into a temple.
[6] Hsüan Tsung refers to the dream that brought Confucius a premonition
of his own death and wonders if he too will receive such a vision.
[7] See Fletcher, *More Gems of Chinese Poetry*, p. 184.
[8] The " Dragon City," a city in Mongolian Tartary.

Shines without ceasing also in the camp of Han.
While the young wife thinks of love,
Her good man yesterday evening thought of her.
Oh ! who will advance the drums and flags and take that
dragon city ?

Inscribed on the Walls of a Courier Station north of Ta-yü [1]
Mountains

by SUNG CHIH-WÊN

IN the tenth moon the wild geese fly south
They carry their migration to a certain point and then return ;
But my travels are never ending
Which day shall I reach my home ?
The floods have just gone down and the river is quiet,
The forest is dark and thick with malarial mists ;
To-morrow morning when I gaze towards my home (from the
top of the pass)
I ought to be able to see the plum blossom along the dykes.

At the Hall of Silence in the Monastery of the Broken Hill
Temple [2]

by CH'ANG CHIEN

I SET out to enter the old monastery in the freshness of early
morning.
The early sun shines down upon high woods,
A winding path leads to this place of quiet.
Here deep among the flowers and trees is the cell of contempla-
tion ;
In the sunlight behind the monastery the birds are enjoying
themselves,

[1] Between Kiangsi and Kuangtung.
[2] See Fletcher, *Gems of Chinese Verse*, pp. 215–16.

The shadows on the pool purge the mind,
All the noise of the world is stilled ;
All I hear are the sounds of the Ch'ing [1] and the monastery bell.

Listening in Szechwan to the monk Chün playing on a Zither [2]

by LI PO

IN Szechwan (I met) a monk clasping a zither in a green brocaded
    cover [3]
Descending the west side of Omei Shan.[4]
When he plucked the strings for me, I listened to the sighing of
    ten thousand pines in mountain valleys ;
My heart was cleansed as with flowing water,
The scattering echoes mingled with the hoar-frost bells.[5]
And I did not perceive that the green hills had grown grey
Nor that autumn clouds had darkened fold upon fold of the
    hills.

Under the Evening Moon thinking of my Younger [6] Brother [7]

by TU FU

THE throb of drums from (distant) garrisons holds up all
    communications,
On the frontiers in autumn one goose is calling ;
From to-night onwards the white hoar frost will fall.

[1] Bronze bowl struck with a muffled stick.
[2] Fletcher, *More Gems*, p. 41.
[3] Actually the term green silk is used to suggest a lute.
[4] Mt. Omei, 11,000 ft. high, sacred to P'u-hsien (Samantabhadra).
The poem perhaps refers to the mythical Po-ya who smashed his guitar
when his one listener died.
[5] In the *Shan-hai Ching* mention is made of nine bells in some vague
fairyland which chime at approaching frost.
[6] One was in Honan, the other in Shensi.
[7] See Fletcher, *Gems of Chinese Verse*, p. 107.

This same moon shines bright on my distant home,
Yet my brothers are all scattered
There is none to ask whether they live or die.
If I send a letter on so long a journey it may not reach its
    destination
All is more difficult now as the war sweeps on.

Written on returning Home to Sung Shan [1]

by WANG WEI

(I WATCH) the long reeds sway [2] to the pure stream
As the carriage goes idly on its way ;
The flowing waters seem to possess a purpose of their own.
As evening (comes I watch) the birds fly home in flocks
(Where) a deserted city looks down on an old ford,
And the glow of the setting sun lies all over the autumn hills.
I have come home to the remote slopes of Sung Shan,
And having come home I shall close my door to the whole
    world.

Saying farewell to the Magistrate Li of T'zŭ Chou [3]

by WANG WEI

FROM ten thousand mountain ravines trees blend with the sky,
From a thousand hills the nightjars are calling ;
In the depths of the hills it rains all night long
From the tops of the trees a hundred little rivulets.
(Where you are in office) the ladies of Han pay tribute with
    Tung cloth, [4]
And the men of Pa [5] litigate over their potato patches.

---

[1] Near Loyang in Honan.   [2] ? line.   [3] In Szechwan.
[4] Ref. to Tso Ssŭ of the Han who wrote about capital taxes of Szechwan.
[5] Part of upper Yangtze valley round Chungking, Szechwan.

Wên,[1] an old man in a foreign land, taught the people
Will you not dare to follow in the footsteps of the men of old ?

Climbing Hsien Shan with my Friends

by MÊNG HAO JAN

ONE generation gives way to another,
The future becomes the present and present merges with the
     past,
Rivers and hills alone preserve their famous features
And here are we once more come to trace them.
The water is low and round " Fish Weir " Island runs shallow
In cold weather the " Dream Pool " is deep ;
Yang's [2] monument is still there,
When one has read the inscription tears wet one's clothes.

Climbing to the Monastery above the Wu Kung Tower and gazing on to the Distance on an Autumn Day

by LIU CH'ANG-CH'ING [3]

SINCE long ago the ancient tower has fallen into decay
Going to it in the autumn it makes me think of the days gone by.
Few pilgrims climb to these crumbling ruins,
Cloud capped precipices brood across deep waters,
The setting sun lingers upon old piled up stones.[4]

---

[1] Wên, a meritorious official who lived in Szechwan in the middle
of the second century B.C. supposed to be the first official to civilize
Szechwan.

[2] Yang Hu (d. A.D. 278) was a Governor of Hsien-yang in the Chin
period. He rose to high office first under Ssŭ-ma Chao and afterwards
under Ssŭ-ma Yen, and received the sobriquet of Gentlemanly General.
On his death the people of Ching-chou put up a memorial stone on Mt.
Hsien, at the sight of which sorrowing people wept so that Tu Yü called
it the Tablet of Tears.

[3] Fletcher, *More Gems*, p. 114.   [4] The ruins of the Wu Kung T'ai.

A cold shiver runs through the empty woods ; [1]
Sadly my thoughts dwell on the relics of the southern dynasty [2]
Only the long river flows on as before.

Saying Farewell to the Governor Li on his Retirement to his country Retreat at Han-yang [3] [4]

by LIU CH'ANG–CH'ING

FINISHED and done with are those days in which you com-
manded that expedition against the south.
Once you led vast armies,
Now you return home dismissed and dispossessed.
Yet in your old age you can look back on the glorious exploits
of the past
(And recollect) how your presence alone kept the Border
Marches in peace and quiet.
You who held your life so lightly sword in hand,
How vast are the stretches of the Chiang and the Han [5]
At sunset where will you be ? [6]

A Poem (title lost) [7]

by LIU SHÊN–HSÜ

THE road's end lies in the white clouds
It is spring for the whole length of the mountain stream ;
The water borne towards me is full of fallen flowers
As I follow the stream it is fragrant all the way.

[1] ? temple grove.
[2] The Ch'ên dynasty, second half of the sixth century.
[3] In Kansu.   [4] More Gems, p. 117.
[5] The Yangtze and the Han rivers meet above Hankow.
[6] Suggesting the twilight of an old man's life with its unknown goal.
[7] Evidently the poet is on his way to visit a scholar in his mountain
retreat.

A quiet doorway faces the mountain path
Where a study lies deep in the shade of the willows;
Wherever you look the sunshine is netted with shadow,
The brilliant contrast flecks my clothes.

On meeting an old Friend from my Home at Chiang-nan [1] by chance at an Inn

by TAI SHU-LUN

IN the autumn sky the moon is full
From the city walls you can see far into the infinite night.[2]
Again we repeat the Chiang-nan meeting
It is really too good to be true.[3]
The wind in the branches startles the hidden magpies,
The dew laden grass numbs the cold insects.
It is meet that travellers seized by home sickness should take
    their fill of deep drinking
But though we strive to keep each other from parting we both
    fear the sound of the morning bell.

Joy at meeting a Cousin again and in Sorrow at the Farewell

by LI YI

AFTER ten years of troubled separation I meet you, now grown
    up.
Startled, I ask you your surname feeling that we are meeting
    for the first time,
But when you tell me your name, then I remember how you
    used to look.
Since we parted great changes have taken place:

---

[1] South of the River.
[2] Lit. ? the city seems enlarged a thousandfold by night.
[3] We suspect it is almost like a dream meeting.

Our talk is not finished till we hear the evening bell;
To-morrow you take the road to Yo Chou [1]
And range upon range of autumn hills will separate us again.

The Temple of the first King [2] of Shu [3]

by LIU YÜ-HSI

DIGNITY and majesty still pervade this place;
Here for a thousand autumns (mankind) has stood in awe.
His power split the land in three;
Once more he re-established the glories of Han, [4]
With the aid of his great minister he was able to establish his
    kingdom,
He bore children but none who could compare with himself.
(The time came when) the former dancing girls of Shu, [5]
    dismissed and ruined,
Went to dance before the palaces of Wei. [6]

Early Autumn

by HSÜ HUN

OUT of the long night floats the music of the clear lute [7]
The western wind stirs the blue tendrils of the creepers;
The last remaining fireflies have come to rest in the green dews,
The first wild goose brushes the Milky Way;
The tall trees are massed in the dawn,
The distance stands out clearer than usual.

[1] On the Tung-t'ing Lake, Hunan.
[2] Liu Pei, who lived in the period of the Three Kingdoms.
[3] See Fletcher, More Gems, pp. 185, 186.
[4] The Wu Chu currency, established by Wu Ti of the Han.
[5] West Szechwan.
[6] Central Shansi.
[7] Once strung with fifty, and later with twenty-five strings.

When the first leaf falls in the Huai-nan [1] district
Then you know there will be waves on the Tung-t'ing [2] lake.

The Cicada [3]

by LI SHANG-YIN

By nature you worship height but it is hard for you to be
    satiated,
I hate to think you too waste your voice in vain ;
At the fifth watch it is intermittent and soon it stops altogether
(Hidden) in a green tree which is indifferent to your presence. [4]
I, a poor official, drifting about like a twig,
See in my garden the weeds are at least rooted out
May I thank you for teaching me the lesson ?
I too with my family will worship purity.

Falling Flowers [5]

by LI SHANG-YIN

From the high pavilions the guests have all gone ;
In the small gardens dishevelled blossoms drop to the ground
Scattered unevenly they lie across the crooked paths,
Far in the distance they dance in the setting sun.
They raise sad thoughts but I dare not brush them away
I strain my eyes after them, but they are determined to go. [6]
My heart (like theirs) yearns for the spring (which is about to
    die)
And I am left with a garment moistened with tears.

[1] Kiangsu.
[2] In Hunan.
[3] An emblem of purity which sips the wind and drinks the dew.
[4] Or perhaps better, " Even if you sit there tucked away in the shade
of the tree, yet you are doomed. Nothing is safe from the world's
cruelty."
[5] Fletcher, *More Gems*, p. 141.
[6] The Chinese poets always talk of the spring going home, i.e. departing.

On the Frontier

by CHANG CH'IAO

THE horn bugles are silent and the autumn passes in peace ;
The warriors rest on the watch towers in the frontier posts.
The spring wind blows across the grave [1] which is always
    green
The white sun goes down over Liang Chou.[2]
In the great wastes of the Gobi desert there are no troops to bar
    the way
Throughout the entire frontier passes travellers come and go.
The temper of the Hun is as unstable as water
Would that it could always flow like this to the south.[3]

The Solitary Goose [4]

by TS'UI T'U

GAGGLE upon gaggle return home beyond the frontier pass and
    are gone.
Why do you wing your way alone ?
Why do you call out for your lost comrades ?
Why do you come so late to your winter pool ?
Against the island mist you pass over low in the darkness.
Though you follow the cold moonlight over the barrier passes,
Will you not meet and fall to the arrow ?
Oh ! Lonely goose, you must be on your guard.

---

[1] The grave of Wang Chao-chün, who was married to a Hsiung-nu
Prince in 33 B.C. Buried across the frontier her grave by tradition
remained green.
  [2] Kansu.   [3] i.e. turn in allegiance to China.
  [4] The accents to the poem are on the words lost, late, low, cold.

The Spring Palace Lament [1]

by TU HSÜN-HÊ

EARLY I was bewitched by my own graces
But now (discarded) I sit at home listless in front of my mirror,
For the road to the imperial favour does not lie in beauty. [2]
To have learnt all the wiles of a concubine how does it avail ? [3]
The wind is warm, birds twitter (in greater numbers),
The sun is high, and the shadows of the flowers are multiplied. [4]
Year by year I find myself (passed over) like the women of
    the stream of Yüeh [5]
Who dreamt of love as they plucked the hibiscus flower. [6]

On climbing the Phœnix Tower at Chin-ling [7] [8]

by LI PO

ONCE on the Phœnix Tower real phœnix wandered,
Now they have gone and the tower is empty but the river flows
    on ; [9]
Flowers and grasses hide the paths of the palaces of Wu [10]
The officials of the Chin [11] dynasty had become old graves.

[1] More Gems, pp. 187, 188.

[2] She has not the money to bribe the eunuchs to bring her existence to the attention of the Emperor.

[3] Probably carries on the sense of the previous line—" does not lie in beauty nor in teaching the women arts of toilet."

[4] The wind and sun of imperial favour which is shared in competition by hoards of concubines.

[5] Hsi Shih was chosen by the King of Wu from the washing girls of Yüeh. Her companions were left behind.

[6] The Emperor's bed-curtains are embroidered with hibiscus flowers.

[7] Nanking.

[8] Fletcher, More Gems, pp. 42, 43.

[9] Phœnix only appear in times of peace and prosperity and good government. The suggestion is that these are hard times.

[10] Kiangsu.   [11] Shansi.

The Three Peaks lie half submerged beneath the blue horizon,
Two streams divide at the white egret island ;
But there are floating clouds which darken the sun [1]
I cannot see Ch'ang-an and that makes me sad.

Made after Continual Rains at the Wang-ch'uan hamlet [2]

by WANG WEI

It has rained for long ; over these lonely woods lingers the
    smoke (of cooking pots) ;
They steam their pulse and bake their millet and send to the
    men working in the last fields.
Over the vast expanse of water-logged fields one white egret
    flies,
In the dark shade of the summer woods a yellow oriole
    calls.
On the hill I practise tranquillity while I gaze at the morning
    hibiscus ; [3]
Under the pines I eat my frugal meal of vegetables and pluck
    the dew-covered sunflower. [4]
An old countryman who has finished jockeying for official
    position,
How is it that the seagulls still have doubts of me ? [5]

[1] Enemies at Court that come between him and imperial favour.

[2] A hamlet on a hill facing the T'ang capital, to-day Sianfu, where
Wang Wei lived with a friend P'ei Ti. He spent his days on the water
strumming on a lute and singing songs.

[3] A shrub whose blossom fades in a day ; a symbol of the fleeting
qualities of life.

[4] The k'uei may mean the mallow or, in Szechwan, the hollyhock ; or
perhaps the seeds of the sunflower.

[5] The seagull is supposed not to be afraid of the hsien, the Bodhisattvas,
but dislikes ordinary mortals. There is a gentle irony in this line.

Songs of Old and Cherished Memory. No. 2

by TU FU

MANY mountains and a myriad ravines converge on the Ching
    Pass.
It was here that Ming-fei [1] was reared and grew up and her
    village exists to-day;
Once she had left the premises of the purple towers [2] she was
    swallowed by the northern deserts,
There only remains her green tomb facing the yellow dusk.
Painting deprived the Emperor of the knowledge of her spring
    wind face;
It is vain to look for the return of her jingling jewels.
There is naught but her ghost wandering under the evening
    moon,
And for ever afterwards her *p'i p'a* [3] makes moan
Making clear the course of her misery in her song.

At Chiang Chou [4] saying Farewell once more to Hsüeh Liu and Liu Pa, supernumerary Officials [5]

by LIU CH'ANG-CH'ING

IN my time of life how could I expect the imperial edict?
All I know about the affairs of state is how to get drunk and
    sing songs.[6]

[1] This poem refers to the fate of Wang Chiang (Chao-chün), a concubine of Yüan Ti (48–33 B.C.), who was presented to a prince of the Hsiung-
nu as a bride. As she had not the means to bribe the court painter
Mao Yen-shou, an unflattering likeness of her was submitted to the
Emperor, who never saw her in the flesh until the audience before her
departure when he was so struck by her beauty that he tried in vain to
redeem her for a camel load of gold. She was supposed to have composed
in her exile a lament on her *p'i p'a* which has survived. Legend has it
that her grave outside the wall for ever remained green.

[2] Forbidden City.   [3] Guitar.   [4] i.e. Kiukiang (Kiangsi.)

[5] He calls them by their small names so he must have known them well.

[6] ? These two lines are impersonal and generic, i.e. " in any man's walk
in life how can he foresee the honour of imperial appointment; in this
world one can only be certain of wine and song."

Above the river the wild geese of Hu [1] pass under a bright moon.
South of the Huai [2] river the leaves fall and the hills of Ch'u [3]
    are more fully revealed ;
I am glad that my place of retreat is near Ts'ang Chou. [4]
Looking back at my reflection, I gaze helplessly at my white hair
I am in my dotage like all who grow old.
I am ashamed that I should trouble you to bid me farewell once
    more and to wish me careful of the wind and waves.

At Ch'ang-sha [5] passing (the site) of the House attributed to Chia I [6]

by LIU CH'ANG-CH'ING

FOR three years you were banished to this tedious place
And you bequeathed to all posterity your " Lament for the
    guest of Ch'u." [6]
Solitary amid the autumn grasses I search where the man once
    lived but now has gone,
I only see the setting sun through the cold woods.
The Emperor Han Wên [7] had many virtues but his benevolence
    was thin.

[1] Mongolia.   [2] Kiangsu.

[3] Hunan.

[4] A seat of hermits and retired scholars in Kiangsi.

[5] Capital of Hunan.

[6] Chia I wrote a "Lament for the guest of Ch'u" to commemorate Ch'ü Yüan, the dragon-boat worthy of the fourth century B.C. and also by implication to state his own sorrows. Chia I lived in the second century B.C. Both of them were victims of official slander and intrigue. Chia I was banished to Chang-sha, became tutor to the Prince of Liang and died within a year. Ch'ü Yüan drowned himself in the Mi-lo River ; at the Dragon-boat Festival held on the fifth day of the fifth moon to search for his body it was fashionable for exiles to comfort themselves by quoting verses of others who had been unjustly banished.

[7] Han dynasty.

The Hsiang [1] waters have no heart, they reck nothing of your
  lament ;
In the desolate hills above the river the leaves are falling.[2]
You unlucky fellow what had you done to bring you here at
  the ends of the world ?

Presented to Mr. P'ei, an Official in the Palace

by CH'IEN CH'I

In the second month the yellow orioles appear in the " upper
  Woods, " [3]
In the spring dawn the imperial city is dark (with foliage) ;
In the palace of " Unending Bliss " the sound of bells fades
  away beyond the flowers,
At the " dragon pool " the colour of the willows is deeper from
  the (spring) rains.
But even the softness of spring cannot dissipate my grief at
  reaching the end of my career.
As stars support the sun so have I never swerved from my
  loyalty to the throne.[4]
Here am I who has offered up my poems [5] for ten years and
  still without success ;
I am ashamed with my white hair to face you with your official
  hat-pins.

[1] Flows into the Tung-t'ing Lake.
[2] Reference to a poem of Sung Yü entitled " The nine arguments " :
" The melancholy air of autumn when trees and grasses start to fall and
change into decay."
[3] Palace gardens.
[4] Lit. " Milky Way constantly hangs sun-supporting heart." There
is the usual comparison between the sun and the emperor.
[5] " Fu " might mean either memorials, examination papers for official
employment, or verses.

Sent to Li Tan and Yüan Hsi

by WEI YING-WU

LAST year here among the flowers we met and parted
To-day the same flowers blossom again and another year has
gone.
The affairs of the world are unsettled and uncertain and difficult
to foretell.
The sadness of my spring thoughts blackens the mind as I sleep
alone.
As I grieve over my bodily ailments I think of my old home
in my native fields,
In my district here there are vagrants and homeless wanderers,
and I am ashamed to take a salary ;
Since you have promised to come and visit me I sit in my
western tower and wonder how many times the moon will
wax and wane before you come.[1]

On Writing, among others, on the Walls of the Taoist Temple of the Wandering Immortal

by HAN HUNG

LOOKING from the terrace of the Immortals into fairyland [2]
The air and the scenery are cold and clear after last night's rain.
At evening the colour of the hills stretches out to the distant
trees of Ch'in,[3]
The noise of washing [4] tells us that autumn has come to the
palaces of Han.

[1] i.e. Come as soon as you can.
[2] The twelve towers of the four cities of Huang Ti, the mythical Yellow
Emperor, who was a Taoist, are used to symbolize a state of unearthly
beauty.   [3] Shensi.
[4] In the palace calendar special days were appointed for changing the
wardrobe to meet the seasons. These were announced in the Court

The chequered shadows of the pines fall upon the surface of
    empty altars,
The fragrant grasses of autumn penetrate the small grottoes (of
    the monastery) :
Why need you seek (for a paradise) outside the world?
Here among men there is also a Cinnabar Hill.[1]

Poem : " On climbing the Tower on the City Wall of Liu
    Chou " [2] sent to the Sub-Prefects of Chang, T'ing, Fêng and
    Lien

by LIU TSUNG-YÜAN

WILD country comes right up to the towers on the city
    wall
The skies are lowering and overcast ; [3]
A violent gust of wind ruffles the hibiscus girdled pond,
Dense rain strikes athwart the creeper-covered wall.
Range upon range of tree-covered hills conceal the distant
    view ;
The river flows crooked as the nine entrails of the human
    body.
All of us live in the territory of the hundred Yüeh [4] where the
    people tattoo their bodies,
A place where letters are hard to come by.

Gazette. It did not matter in fact whether the weather was seasonable.
This passage tells us that the summer clothes have been washed prior to
being put away for the autumn.
    [1] A fairyland where legend says the immortals lived ; the isles of the
blest where there was no night and always day.
    [2] Kuangsi.
    [3] Lit. " The ocean of heaven entertains sad thoughts as vast as
itself."
    [4] Kuangtung and Kuangsi were only brought under the central
government in T'ang times. The Cantonese still call themselves men of
T'ang, not of Han.

At the Hill of the Western Fort thinking of Ancient Days

by LIU YÜ-HSI

WHEN Wang Chün's [1] high-decked war junks came down from
    Yi Chou [2]
There was an end to the royal majesty of Chin-ling.[1]
A thousand chains fell to the bottom of the river,
A single flag of surrender came out of the rocky headland.
How often does one look back with regret on the events of
    the past ?
Yet the mountain passes are as before and lie athwart the cold
    flowing river ;
To-day the four seas have become one family,
And the old forts all deserted are overgrown with autumn reeds.

The Deer Park [3]

by WANG WEI [4]

AN empty hill, and no one in sight
But I hear the echo of voices.[5]
The slanting sun at evening penetrates the deep woods
And shines reflected on the blue lichens.

[1] Wang Chün was a general in the period of the Three Kingdoms who
in A.D. 279, on behalf of Chin, marched against Wu and captured the
capital Chin Ling (Nanking) which was protected by iron chains across
the river. Wang Chün sent down rafts manned by a few experienced
sailors and loaded with dummy soldiers and inflammables who fired the
chains, melted them, and the way was open to Chin Ling.

[2] Szechwan.   [3] See *Gems*, p. 123.

[4] It was Su Tung-p'o who said of Wang Wei " his pictures were poems,
his poems pictures."

[5] The woods are so thick that woodcutters and herdsmen are hidden.

The Lodge amid the Bamboos [1]

by WANG WEI

ALONE I sit surrounded by deep bamboo groves;
I thrum my lute and hum my songs,
In the deep woods no one is aware of me
But the bright moon comes to look at me and I respond.

Lasting Affection [2]

by WANG WEI

THE red bean [3] grows in the south,
When spring comes how many tendrils does it put forth?
I want you to pick a few for me
Because they stand for loving thoughts and fond remembrance.

Miscellaneous Verse [4]

by WANG WEI

SINCE, Sir, you come to me straight from the old country
You ought to know the affairs of my native place:
On the day you left had the winter plum put forth flower in
    front of the gauze-curtained window?

---

[1] See *More Gems*, p. 213.   [2] See *More Gems*, p. 108.

[3] The red bean known as the " mutually lovesick " grows in Kwang-tung.   Commentator says it grows several feet high, has leaves like bird's wings, flowers that from the top look like butterflies.   The flower is white, pink or red.   The beans flat, half red and black.   A woman is supposed to have died from love under this tree.   It is used for love potions in Canton.

[4] *More Gems*, p. 110 (a bad translation).

Farewell to Ts'ui Chiu

by P'EI TI

WHEN you go back to the deep ravines and shallow valleys of
　　the hills
You must thoroughly explore the beauty of scar and fell;
Don't go and copy the Wu-ling man [1]
Who for such a short time went to live in the land of the source
　　of the Peach Flower Spring.

Anchoring at Night on the Chien-tê [2] River [3]

by MÊNG HAO-JAN

I MOVE my boat and anchor in the mists off an islet;
With the setting sun the traveller's heart grows melancholy
　　once more.
On every side is a desolate expanse of water;
Somewhere the sky comes down to the trees
And the clear water reflects a neighbouring moon.

Night Thoughts

by LI PO

IN front of my bed there is bright moonlight
I think there must be hoar frost on the ground;
I raise my head and gaze at the bright moon,
Lowering it I think of the old country.

---

[1] Reference to a poem by Tao Yüan-ming, called " The Source of the
Peach Flower Spring "—the hero of the story found the land of the
immortals came back but could not return.　The suggestion is " don't be
so stupid as to come back if you get there."　Some Chinese commentators
prefer to interpret it " I want to go with you next time, so don't forget
the way."

[2] Chekiang.　　　　　　　　　　　　[3] See More Gems, p. 152.

On Playing the Lute [1]

by LIU CH'ANG CH'ING

COLD and clear sounds the seven-stringed lute
Softly strummed to the air of the " Wind in the Winter Pines ; "[2]
Although I love these old tunes
Nowadays very few people play them.

Listening to the Chêng [3]

by LI TUAN

As she sounds the chêng she tightens or loosens the pegs
One white hand is drawn over the sounding board.
She wishes Mr. Chou [4] could come and see her
Then she would deliberately play a few wrong notes.

In the Manner of the Jade Tower [5]

by CH'UAN TÊ-YÜ

LAST night I dreamt that someone untied my girdle,
To-day the lucky spider [6] swings itself before me.
It is no longer fitting to neglect my cosmetics,
It must be time that my old washing block is coming back home.

[1] *More Gems*, p. 116.
[2] Perhaps " Wind blowing cold in the pines."
[3] An instrument played with a plectrum.
[4] Chou Yü was a good-looking young man who lived in the period of the Three Kingdoms and was a great connoisseur of music. When a false note was struck he would look sternly at the performer.
[5] The Jade Tower manner suggests a certain elegant indelicacy.
[6] Pun on her good fortune, or does it refer to an illicit lover who is now clearing out ? Giles translates the passage : " the morning the spider (her lover) has fled."

Snow on the River [1,2]

by LIU TSUNG-YÜAN

On a thousand hills all bird life is cut off,
On ten thousand paths there is no trace of human footsteps;
In a lonely boat the old man with the bamboo hat and cape
Sits by himself fishing the river in the winter snow. [3]

The Travelling Palace [4]

by YÜAN CHÊN

Empty and falling down is the ancient travelling palace,
The palace flowers put forth their red blooms in silent neglect.
Inside a white-headed palace woman
Idly mumbles of the (glorious) days of Hsüan Tsung.

Inviting Mr. Liu Shih-chiu

by PO CHÜ-I

I have " green ant " [5] newly fermented wine
My little stove of red earth is ready (for heating the wine);
Evening comes and the heavens threaten snow
Can you not come and drink a cup or so with me?

---

[1] *More Gems*, p. 153.

[2] The author writes this after he had been sacked from his official job
and found the world cold and bleak.

[3] ? " Fishing for winter snow." If he was a Buddhist philosopher he
would fish without a hook.

[4] These travelling palaces were sometimes very elaborate. One was
constructed each stage of the journey between Peking and Jehol and
others on the way to the imperial tombs.

[5] This seems a strange name for a wine.

A Song of the Frontier [1]

by LU LUN

With his Chin p'u-ku [2] eagle-feather arrows
And his Mao-hu [2] swallow-tail brocade pennants
Alone (the general) stands to give his latest orders,
And the whole camp answers in one voice.
The trees are dark and the grasses rustle in the wind,
That night the general draws his bow ;
When the day dawns he searched for the white feathers (of his
    arrows)
And found them stuck in the fissures of a rock. [3]
The moon is obscured
The wild geese fly high,
The Tartar general at night slinks away.
Lightly equipped we ride our horses in pursuit
And swords and bows are covered with snow.
In our field camp we spread out awnings and a noble feast,
We congratulate ourselves on our return (from the defeat) of
    Ch'iang and Yung.
We drink our fill and dance in full accoutrements ;
The thunder of our drums echoes among the hills and streams.

[1] The first stanza describes the panoply of war. The second the
general's courage. The third, the march against the Tartars. The
fourth, the rejoicings after their defeat.
[2] The Tso-chüan describes Chin-p'u-ku as a name of any superior
arrow. The Mao-hu pennants were a kind of banner.
[3] It would appear that the general was so frightened by the rustle in
the grass that he fired at a venture. To us it suggests panic, but to the
Chinese courage. The reference is to a certain general Li Kuang of the
Han, who is recorded in the Shih chi to have shot at a rock in the
dusk in mistake for a tiger and to have found two arrows embedded in
it next day.

Going down to Chiang-ling [1] [2]
or
Setting off in the early Morning from Po Ti [3]
by LI PO

IN the morning we say farewell to Po Ti among the flowing
 clouds ;
It is a thousand miles to Chiang-ling but we do it in a day : [4]
On the two banks the monkeys call without ceasing ;
The light boat has already passed through range upon range of
 hills.

On meeting Li Kuêi-nien [5] south of the River in the South
Country
by TU FU

IN the old days I saw you at the palace of the Prince of Ch'i, [6]
And I often heard you before the halls of Ts'ui Chiu. [7]
South of the Yangtze it is still peaceful and the scenery is good,
And now in the time of falling blossoms [8] I meet you once
 again.

A Moonlight Night
by LIU FANG-P'ING

IN the depths of the night the moonlight floods one side [9] of the
 houses of men,
The Great Bear has dropped crosswise and the Southern Dipper
 is aslant ;

[1] Hupei.   [2] *Gems*, p. 26.   [3] Szechwan.
[4] Going down the Yangtze with the current.
[5] A street-singer famous before the revolution of An Lu-shan.
[6] A prince of the royal house of Hsüan Tsung.
[7] A bosom friend of Hsüan Tsung and his chief private secretary.
[8] Falling blossom time = " the autumn of the dynasty," " the autumn
of age," " the autumn of the year."
[9] It is difficult to decide here whether the passage means that the moon
is only half-full or that its beams light up only one-half of every house,
the rest being in shadow.

This evening one really feels that the spring air is warm,
For the first time the sound of insects penetrates my window of
green gauze.

A Palace Song

by KU KʻUANG

FROM the Jade Tower half-way up to heaven floats the sound of
songs to the *shêng*,[1]
The gay laughter of the palace girls comes down to us on the
wind.
The Hall of the Moon casts its shadow and one hears the
evening clepsydra ;
The crystal blind is rolled up and we seem to be quite close to
the Milky Way.[2]

Black Coat Lane [3]

by LIU YÜ-HSI

AT the " Red Black " Bridge the wild grasses flower,
At the mouth of the " Black Coat " Lane sets the slanting sun.
Of old times swallows flew before the halls of Wang and
Hsieh [4]
Now they enter the houses of the common people.

---

[1] The *shêng* is a reed organ with thirteen pipes, the model of an organ :
said to have been introduced into the West from China.   Tradition says
the player on the *shêng* must be pure, otherwise he will die.   Only Taoist
priests are supposed to play it.

[2] i.e. The Autumn River.   Probably here suggests the Imperial
presence which the ladies hope is close at hand.

[3] A reference to past glories of a smart suburb of Nanking which had
sunk to a slum.

[4] The sons of the old aristocratic houses of Wang Tao and Hsieh An,
since they wore black clothes were nicknamed the swallows.

The Spring Song

by LIU YÜ-HSI

THE girl with the newly painted face comes down from the red
  tower
She steals sadly like a ray of spring sunlight into the deeply
  locked court,[1]
She walks to the middle of the courtyard to count the flowers ;
A dragonfly alights upon the top of her jade comb.

Bestowed upon a Courtesan of the Palace [2]

by CHANG HU

STREAKS of moonlight pass through the trees within the For-
  bidden City,
Her seductive eyes dwell upon the nesting heron ;
Leaning aslant in the shadows of the lantern she plucks out a jade
  hairpin
And picks at the flame to save the flying moths.

A Palace Ode [3]

by CHU CH'ING-YÜ

LONELY and desolate, though it is in the season of the flowers,
  for the palace door shut
Two fair ladies (stand) together on the jasper balcony.
They keep their feelings to themselves although they would like
  to gossip about palace affairs,
For they dare not speak as a parrot is set before the door.

[1] The palace being severely exclusive, the spring sunshine is, as it were,
securely locked away like the imperial concubines within its precincts,
and becomes like them wistful and sad.
  [2] Ladies from the " Springlike Courtyard," very different and far
superior to ordinary prostitutes.
  [3] An allegorical poem illustrating the poet's own disappointment in
official life.

Sent at the time of a Recent Examination to Mr. Chang of the Water Board [1]

by CHU CH'ING-YÜ

LAST night the red candles were snuffed out in the bridal
    chamber
To-morrow the bride will pay her respects to her in-laws in the
    Ancestral Hall ;
Her toilet completed, she asks her husband in a low voice
Whether her eyebrows are painted in a fashionable style.

The Red Cliffs [2]

by TU MU

A SNAPPED spearhead is found in the sand but the iron is not yet
    disintegrated ;
I take it and rub it and clean it and recognize the style of a
    former dynasty.
If the east wind had not come to the assistance of Chou Lang
In spring at T'ung Ch'iao, Ts'ao T'sao would have assuredly
    locked up the two ladies Ch'iao. [3]

[1] The metaphor of the bridal chamber is compared to the examination
hall. The scholar is compared to a bride. The examination to her toilet.
Her husband to the examiner. The poet was sending his recent essay
at the examination to Mr. Chang to see. At the same time he sent the
accompanying poem.

[2] In S. Hupei the Yangtze, the scene of Ts'ao T'sao's defeat by fire-ships
in the Three Kingdoms.

[3] Chou Yü was sent by Chu-ko Liang with fire-ships to defeat Ts'ao
T'sao. The two girls, one of them the daughter of Chou, were well
known for their looks. Ts'ao T'sao said it was his ambition if he defeated
Chou Yü to take the ladies Ch'iao and lock them up in a bronze bird
tower (which he would build) " to toy with them in the evening of his
years."

The Garden of the Golden Valley

by TU MU

THE splendours and luxuries (of the Tsin dynasty) are scattered
and lost along with the fragrant dust ;
Yet the waters still flow on their passionless way and the flowers
still bloom in spring.
At dusk the east wind resents the calls of the (roosting) birds [1]
And the falling flowers remind me of the girl who threw herself
from the tower.[2]

Written in the Evening Rain to a Friend in the North

by LI SHANG–YIN

YOU ask me when I come home again ? I answer, I am not
certain when I can come ;
In the Pa Hills [3] the evening rain swells the autumn pools.
When shall we sit down again together to snuff the candles in
the western window
And talk about the rain on the hills of Pa ?

There is a Reason

by LI SHANG–YIN

THE screen that hides my bed is painted with clouds beautiful
beyond compare,
Yet in the Phœnix City though the winter is finished I dread the
spring nights ;

[1] A more literal translation, " the sun sets ; an east wind blows ; sadly
the birds call."
[2] Lü-chu. The " green pearl," a concubine of Shih Ch'ung, who,
when sought after by a great official who wished to take her by force,
committed suicide by leaping from a tower. See Giles, *B. Dict.*, No. 1709.
[3] North-east of Tung-hsiang Hsien, Szechwan.

84

For married without affinity to a high official, I am all alone ;
Paying me scant justice he throws aside the scented coverlet and
goes off to the early morning leveé.

The Jasper Pond [1] [2]

by LI SHANG-YIN

WHEN Hsi Wang Mu opens the silken curtained windows on to
the Jasper Pond,
The song of the " Yellow Bamboos " [3] moves the whole earth
to sadness.
Although he had eight horses that could travel thirty thousand
miles a day
How was it that Mu Wang did not come back again ?

Sad Thoughts on a Jasper Lute

by WÊN T'ING-YÜN

COOL are the bamboo mats and silver white the bed, but dreams
will not come ;
The green skies are like waters and the evening clouds steal
lightly by ;
A wild goose calls in the distance as it passes over the Hsiao
and Hsiang,[4]
The twelve towers [5] are bathed in the light of a bright moon.

[1] The abode of Hsi Wang Mu, the Queen of the Taoist fairyland.

[2] A Chinese commentary refers to the poem as " fairy rubbish."

[3] The reference is to a mythical King of Chou, Mu Wang, who rode
up to Hsi Wang Mu in a chariot drawn by eight horses and was given
the peach of immortality. On the way most of his guard died of ex-
posure and so he composed a lament, " the Yellow Bamboo." When
he came back he planted the kernel of the peach that Hsi Wang Mu had
given him, but it did not take gladly to the air of this world.

[4] Hsiao and Hsiang are two rivers in southern Hunan, which unite
their waters.

[5] The twelve towers is an allusion to the towers built by the Yellow
Emperor to receive the spirits.

A Portrait of Chin-ling [1]

by WEI CHUANG

OVER the river where the reeds bend close packed to the driven
    rain
The Shades of the Six Dynasties pass like a dream,
While a desolate bird sings.
The weeping willows follow the city towers, careless of the
    vanished glories of the past
And enclose as of old the moats for ten *li* in a misty cage.

The Ballad of Lung Hsi [2]

by CH'ÊN T'AO

SWEARING they would sweep away the Hsiung-nu,
They took no thought for their own bodies.
Five thousand men clad in sable and silks [3] fell in the Tartar
    desert.
Pity their bones with no resting place strewn on the banks of
    the Wu-ting Ho ; [4]
But still in spring in the women's apartments they dream of the
    men that went away. [5]

---

[1] The poem is a lament for the vanished glories of the capital. Chin-
ling = Nanking ; the poem was no doubt written on a painting of that
city.

[2] Kansu.

[3] The sable and silks are really only the fur coats worn by Chinese
soldiers when fighting in the cold border regions of the north-west.

[4] There was a river of that name in Shensi.

[5] Alternative reading, " But still in spring they visit in dreams the wives
they have left behind."

86

Occasional Stanzas

ANONYMOUS

IT is near the time of " Cold Food " [1] ; rain makes the grasses
  grow.
The young wheat waves in the wind and the willows cast their
  shadows on the dykes.
It is the same with all of us who have a home but cannot go back
  to it.
Do not visit us, nightjar, [2] nor let us hear your call.

A Song of Wei Ch'êng [3]

by WANG WEI

THE morning rains of Wei Ch'êng moisten the light dust,
At the guest house the willow buds are green.
Let me beg of you to drink with me one more cup of wine
When you get to the west of Yang Pass there will be no old
  friends.

Autumn Evening Song

by WANG WEI

THE cassia tree in the moon [4] sheds its brightness, the autumnal
  dew is light ;
Although her light robe is thin she has not changed it ;

---

[1] The story of the supposed origin of this custom of eating cold food
on the festival is very well known. Doubtless it is really the Chinese
version of a world-wide custom of extinguishing all fires once a year
and lighting the " new fire."

[2] The nightjar is supposed to say " home again." There is an old
legend about an exiled king whose spirit entered into a nightjar.

[3] In Shensi. The poem is also well known as the Yang-kuan Ch'u and
is taken as a type of farewell poem.

[4] This phrase is used to describe the eighth moon in particular, when
it begins to wax. Here it also suggests autumn.

On a silver lute she strums diligently all night long
For she is nervous and does not want to go back to an empty
room.

Beyond the Border Passes

by WANG CHIH-HUAN

IN the distance the Yellow River loses itself in white clouds
A lonely [1] stretch of wall trails away among topless hills ;
Why must the Tartar flute [2] wrong the willows (by playing a
willow song) [3]
For the spring wind cannot enter the Jade Door Pass ? [4]

The tune " Clear Happiness " [5]

by LI PO

THE clouds make me think of her trailing garments and the
flowers of her face ;
The spring wind brushes the balustrade where she was enclosed,
The dew lies heavy on the flowers.

---

[1] Lit. The " lonely city "—the reference being to a section of the Great
Wall among the mountains.   The Great Wall is known in China as the
ten thousand li long city.

[2] The Tartar flute is said to have been invented in the reign of Han
Wu Ti.

[3] A well-known tune played on the Tartar flute was a song of farewell,
called the Willow-plucking Song.

[4] The civilizing influence of China does not reach beyond the Tartar
passes.

[5] This poem seems to be placed by the author in the mouth of the
Emperor Hsüan Tsung ; the theme is the beauty of Yang Kuei-fei who
was as lovely as the flowers that clustered around her. But the con-
templation of the flowers brings sadness as well as joy, because they will
soon be scattered by the spring breezes.   Yang Kuei-fei too was one day
to lie dead and dishonoured.

If I may not see her at the top of the Hill of Many Jewels,[1] I
    shall meet her beneath the moon of the terrace of jade.
I am seduced by a spray of red blossom fragrant with dew,
Loneliness like that of the spirit of the clouds and rain inspires
    a hopeless heart-broken longing.[2]
Let me ask who in the Han palace was to be compared with her?
Not even the " flying swallow "[3] in her grand toilet, for all her
    languishing beauty.
The peony and her beauty which overthrew a kingdom were
    both dear to my heart.[4]
When the Imperial eyes gazed on her then my pleasure was
    bound to her smile.
The spring wind brings me a limitless sorrow
When I think where to the north of the fragrant Aloes pavilion
    she leant upon the balustrade.

On a Summer Day in the Southern Pavilion thinking of Hsin Ta

by MÊNG HAO-JAN

THE glow over the hills dies suddenly in the west,
In the east the moon rises slowly over the lake.
I loosen my hair and catch the cool evening breeze,
Opening the door on to the balcony I lie down and take my
    ease.
The wind brings in the smell of fragrant lotus
The dew-drops from the bamboos drip to a music of their own.

[1] The Jade Mountain was where Hsi Wang Mu lived. The meaning
of the two lines is that Yang Kuei-fei's beauty was such that in the Emperor's eyes she seemed to belong not to this world but to the fairyland
of Hsi Wang Mu. He is looking forward to meeting her again in one
of the Taoist paradises.

[2] Prince Hsiang of Ch'u and dreamt he met the fairy of the River Lo
and had relations (clouds and rain) with her.

[3] A court beauty of the reign of Han Ch'ing Ti.

[4] The Emperor Hsüan Tsung.

I should like to strike my lute to a ringing tune
But alas ! there is no one here who would understand.
My thoughts are stirred as I cherish the memories of old friends :
In the middle of the dark (night) I am troubled by longing
    dreams.

On saying Farewell to my Daughter Yang [1]

by WEI YING-WU

I AM in misery all the day long
As I think of the long road that lies before the traveller.
To-day my daughter leaves me
Going up the big river against the current in a light boat.
You have felt the bitterness of having had no one to trust
So I brought you up with added care and tenderness.
It is proper that the old should not hold the young
But when they have to part the tears will flow without stopping.
As for me, my heart is overcome by sadness
But since you should go it is hard to retain you.
From the time you were small you have lacked a mother's
    counsel,
I am anxious as to how you may serve your mother-in-law.
Fortunately the doors of those you enter are considerate,
Benevolence and numerous kindnesses await you
So there need be no cause for complaint.
We are a poor family but not unworthy ; [2]
But how could I have given you an adequate dowry ?
Be dutiful and submissive and follow the right way of women
In all your actions obey the rules of conduct.
This is the morning of our parting ;
How many years may pass before I see you again ?

[1] The girl was surnamed Yang, and appears to have been his adopted
daughter.
[2] Possibly—" to the poor thrift is a thing to be valued."

At home heretofore I lived carefree,
But meeting with this sorrow I find it hard to bear.
On my return home I shall see your young sister
With tears flowing freely and her hat-strings loose.

Gazing at the Moon and cherishing Thoughts of a distant Friend

by CHANG CHIU-LING

ABOVE the sea the bright moon is born
From the horizon it lights up the whole length of heaven,
Passionately I mourn your absence throughout the night
All night long my loving thoughts arise ;
I put out my candle in compassion for the light of the
     moon
I put on my cloak because the dew is heavy ;
As I am sorry I cannot fill my hands with moonlight and give
     it to you
I go back to bed and dream of meeting you again.

Resting on my Journey at the foot of the Pei-ku [1] Hill

by WANG WAN

THE travellers' road winds below blue hills,
The boat goes on into the green waters.
Flat marshes stretch between broad shores
The wind is on our bows and a single sail holds the horizon.
As the night dies the sun comes up over the water,
Spring on the river has broken up the old year.
How can a letter be sent home ?
Ah ! (could I catch) those homing geese passing over to the
     borders of Lo-yang.

[1] Kiangsu.

Sending off a Friend [1]

by LI PO

LOOKING north of the city you see a line of blue hills,
Sparkling water flows past the eastern gate.
Here we part once for all ;
A solitary waterweed [2] drifts off into the distance.
When I think of the wandering clouds you will come back into
    my thoughts
Sunset will bring with it memories of you.
We part now with a wave of the hand ; as we turn our horses
    they neigh farewell.

With the width of Heaven between us thinking of Li Po [3]

by TU FU

A CHILL wind springs up from the horizon,
What are your thoughts now I wonder ?
When will the wild geese arrive ?
Rivers and lakes are big with autumn floods
Your literary compositions are a foe to your success,
The ghouls are gleeful when people (like you) pass by [4]
I fear your path corresponds to that of the " aggrieved spirit." [5]
Throw a poem to him into the Mi-lo River.[6]

---

[1] Obata, p. 94, Fletcher, *More Gems*, p. 7.
[2] A very attractive reading is " solitary sail "—unfortunately the last line indicates horseback.
[3] Fletcher, *More Gems*, p. 99.
[4] i.e. jealous officials lie in wait to do you harm.
[5] Allusion to Ch'ü Yüan, whose death is celebrated by the dragon-boat festival. He had a similar experience.
[6] Near Ch'ang-sha. Hunan.

On passing the Hsiang-chi Monastery [1]

by WANG WEI

I DID not know the way to the Hsiang-chi Monastery;
For several miles I wandered among cloudy peaks
On an untrodden path that ran among ancient trees.
In the depths of the hills whence comes the sound of that ancient
     bell ?
The murmur of water swallowing great boulders (comes to my
     ears),
The cold colours of the sunset light the green pines.
Along the way everything is indistinct in mist
And the pool is dry by the crooked path.
Here peaceful meditation subdues the dragon of desire.

Verses on approaching Tung-t'ing sent to Mr. Chang, the Official

by MÊNG HAO-JAN

IN the eighth month the waters of the lake are smooth
Enveloping the void they merge into the sky ;
Vapour rises from the Yün-mêng Tsê [2]
In the ripples tremble the reflections of Yo-yang [3] city.
I wish to cross but there is no boat nor oar to take me ; [4]
Idling with no fixed purpose I am ashamed to think of the men
     of old.
I sit and enjoy the fishermen, how I admire that fishing feeling ?

Made at Chinese New Year

by LIU CH'ANG-CH'ING

AT New Year I am smitten with thoughts of my own village.
In the far-off boundaries of the empire I weep alone
Old but still in official harness.

[1] Fletcher, *More Gems*, p. 107.
[2] A marsh fifty miles south of An-lu Hsien.   [3] Hunan.
[4] The fact that he cannot get a boat seems to suggest to him that he
cannot get back to office.

Spring's homecoming is earlier than that of the exile
Living with monkeys in the mountains all the year round,
Sharing with the river willows the trailing mists.
I am like the tutor of Ch'ang-sha [1]
How many years must pass before I return?

Seeing a Friend home North after the Troubles

by SSŬ-K'UNG SHU

IN troubled times we went south together
Now it is peaceful you go back alone
In exile you have grown white hairs.
In our old home you will see the green hills,
In bright moonlight you will pass the ruined fort
Under the stars you will sleep at the old barrier pass.
[2] Here winter birds are scattered over barren wastes
And everywhere I look sad beauty holds sway.

Staying at an Inn

by TU MU

As I stay at the inn alone
My fancy runs in a sad vein.
In the cold light of the lamp I think of old days
(The cry of) a stray goose disturbs my melancholy sleep,
Dreams of my distant home steal the morning hours.

[1] Chia I, a native of Lo-yang who lived in the second century B.C., whose talents were brought to the notice of the Emperor Wei Ti of the Han dynasty. He was so young that the Court officials were jealous of him and caused him to be banished to be a tutor to a Prince of Liang at Ch'ang Sha in Hunan where he died.

[2] These last two lines may refer to the country round the old home, in which case the sense would run—" Where winter birds and barren wastes will everywhere be the accompaniment to your sad countenance."

The family letters come only at intervals of years
Yet o'er the breadth of the river moon and mist are beautiful,
And at the gate of the inn I see a fisherman has tied up his
 boat.[1]

Passing by Hua-yin [2]

by TS'UI HAO

THE towering heights of T'ai Hua look down upon Hsien-yang,[3]
Above the sky the three peaks (stand out)
(Even the Hsien) [4] could not cut them down.
In front of the temple of Wu Ti the clouds are about to part
Above the Hsien's palm [5] the rain first clears ;
River and mountain to the north pillow the perilous pass of
 Ch'in,
The courier route to the west leads on to the plains of Han ;
I ask the strangers at the roadside who seek for fame and profit [6]
Why they do not linger here and learn how to live ?

[1] i.e. That this is a fit place for a recluse. The life of the fisherman
and the woodcutter became the emblems of the hermit. But here the
author would seem to be emphasizing his desolation by throwing into
relief a contrasting picture.

[2] See Fletcher, *More Gems*, pp. 174, 175. A district in Shensi.

[3] Shensi.

[4] i.e. Immortals. Perhaps " men cannot whittle them away " or
" carved out by no human hand," makes sense.

[5] The Hsien palm is a naked scar on the cliff.

[6] The road was a highway between Lo-yang and Ch'ang-an.

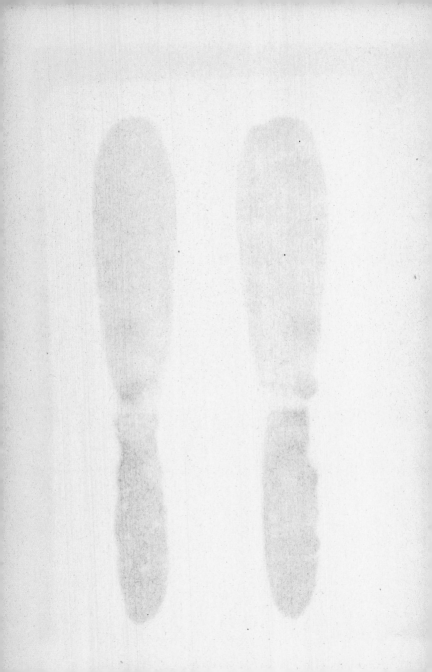